You Are In The
Right Place

You Are In The Right Place

By O.A. Bud Ham

The White Feather Press

First edition
First Printing, 1995
Second Printing, 2014

Illustrations: Retta Va Springer
Cover design: Barry Eisenach, Phoenix Design
Book design: Bob Schram, Bookends

Library of Congress Catalog Card Number 95-61128

ISBN 978-0-9646397-4-4 (paperback)

A c k n o w l e d g m e n t s

To John Bradshaw for challenging me

To Bruce Millar for fifteen years of gentle encouragement

To Don and Donna Sattem for insisting and enabling

To my client friends whose patience with my mind wanderings allowed clarification and my own learning

To Jandy Ham-Dugan and Carol Core for finishing touches

To Judy Ham for her unselfishness

To Dan Ham for motivating my search

Dedication

to Daniel Charles Ham
& Alonzo Ham

Contents

F o r e w o r d

by John Bradshaw

I believe a foreword should tell you more about a book's author than about the text itself. Ideas stand on their own merit or demerit. But ideas are less motivating to me if their presenter does not embody them in his or her own life.

I can honestly say that Bud Ham walks the walk that he talks. I have known Bud for almost fifteen years and I assure you he's the genuine article. His spirituality, so often hidden in males, is what is most apparent about Bud.

Bud embodies what he talks about in this book. He always seems to be in "the right place." He speaks with certainty and passion, but never with grandiosity or righteousness. It does not take long to know what Bud stands for, but he's also curious and open to new learning. His spirituality is practical and down-to-earth. It is rooted in Bud's heartfelt trust in a still small voice within himself he calls God. Bud believes that if we make our choices according to this inner voice, we will live without fear. Fear is unquestionably the root of human suffering, and the promise of a life without fear is incredibly challenging.

Some might call the reliance on an inner voice too subjective and dangerous. I think Bud would agree, and that's why he refuses to live without the feedback from a supportive community. Community ensures that our interpretations of the loving source of our lives is not our own contaminated subjectivity.

Bud's first level of community support is his family. They model the kind of democratically shared power and love that I most believe in. In addition to his family, Bud networks with thousands of dentists who are committed to holistic health.

Read this book and test for yourself the power of Bud's brand of spirituality. With the promise of a life free of fear, you can't afford not to try it. Trust me. You won't be disappointed.

AN AUTOBIOGRAPHICAL SKETCH

SUMMER SEEMED TO LAST FOREVER. My older sister and two cousins, with whom I had enjoyed the seemingly endless sunny days, were back in school. Now I played alone.

I overheard a conversation between my mother, my aunt, and my grandmother Ham. I heard my aunt say, "I know times are tough, but a cake isn't enough. A boy has to have a present on his birthday!"

A few minutes later I saw my aunt drive my grandfather's Willys Knight sedan toward town. Aunt Edna had a part-time job at the Snow White Laundry.

That evening at supper, just before the five candles were lit on my birthday cake, I opened two small packages. In one was a toy airplane; in the other a car. I felt very privileged to receive the toys and played with them for hours at a time on the warm days before winter came.

My mother was Nellie. She was dominated by my father, Lonnie, in most situations, in the long run she proved to be the stronger. She seldom went to church, but she had a quiet faith in God that helped her maintain a beautiful peacefulness and an optimistic outlook throughout her life.

I had often heard the stories about how my father and grandfather Rupp (Nellie's father) had failed at ranching near Glenwood Springs, Colorado. I never tired of hearing my father tell the stories about the fierceness of the winters, how black bears sometimes chased the dogs onto the porch of the ranch house at night, and how he and his family survived eating potatoes and venison. I was proud of my father, especially when he told of how he had killed six deer one winter with seven bullets, fired from Grandpa Rupp's .303 caliber British rifle.

My father would sometimes talk for hours about the ranch, how he had trained a horse named Blue to gallop in place, how they had drained a beaver pond to capture the trout it held for a change from the monotonous diet of venison. I also loved to hear the story of how my father had brought home a puppy in his coat pocket one cold winter day. The dog, Ring, still lived with us. I dearly loved that big dog, and it was obvious my dad did too.

I was born Oscar Alonzo "Buddy" Ham, on the ranch, September 17, 1932. Two weeks later the ranch was given back to the bank and the two families moved back to southern Colorado. My dad felt fortunate to get a job at the Ford garage. He was the all night man, working from 6:00 P.M. to 6:00 A.M. seven days a week. His ability as a good mechanic was well known throughout the area. Times were indeed hard, but there was enough to eat and love was in good supply.

After the foreclosure Grandpa and Grandma Rupp and their three youngest children moved back to the homestead ranch, which they still owned. It was located about twenty miles from Florence where I grew up. Making a living on this ranch was possible, but very difficult. Grandpa often took a day job somewhere else.

Grandpa Rupp was a small man, but very strong. He was never sick a day in his life. As a young man he was a stagecoach driver for the Tallyho Stage Coach Company, which operated between Cripple Creek and Florence, Colorado. In his later years, when he became more talkative, he graphically described how the stage was held up and robbed several times when he was the driver. He said stagecoach robberies were so common they never appeared on the front pages of the newspapers.

Grandma Rupp was a very loving woman and the most even-tempered person in the family. If she ever raised her voice or said a cross word, no one remembered it. She and her family had come to southern Colorado from Indian Territory, now Oklahoma, in a covered wagon when she was seven years old. It was occasionally alluded to, but never openly discussed, that her mother was an Indian. Her physical features strongly suggested Native American heritage. It was well known in the family that she would not discuss her background. No one knew for sure which tribe Grandma's mother might have been from. She was tall, like the Sioux, who had been forced to move to Indian Territory near the end of the Indian Wars.

My other set of grandparents, Grandpa and Grandma Ham, lived on the small farm next door to my family. Grandpa was the undisputed spiritual leader of the family. He was very faithful to his beliefs but he never pressed them on anyone. He was an honest man and respected by all who knew him. Grandma Ham was the strongest member of the clan. She never hesitated to tell anyone what they should or ought to do. She was also the family doctor, the midwife for the community when the real doctor couldn't come, and without question the hardest working person in the family. She expected others to work hard too and told them so.

I was never a great student, but I was a good student through the seventh grade. Two things happened in my twelfth and thirteenth years that greatly changed my life, especially my social and school life. When I was twelve my brother, Dan, was born. Dan was severely afflicted with cerebral palsy. I was just beginning to cope successfully with that difficulty when my life and equilibrium were torn asunder a second time. My father fell from grace—fell very hard. He had an affair with another woman for a year. Many nights I listened to my mother cry herself to sleep. My father and I were not friends again for over twenty years.

These two traumatic events shattered my belief that I was part of an honorable family. I started avoiding all but the most necessary contact with my peer group. From the eighth grade through graduation from high school I was at or near the bottom of my class academically. I no longer felt comfortable around other people. I only experienced peace when I was alone. So I withdrew and spent as much time as possible in the solitary pursuits of hunting, trapping, fishing, and reading.

A few months after graduating from high school in 1950, I joined the United States Marine Corps. As it turned out I didn't know anyone in the Corps. To me this was a Godsend. At last I was free of being around anyone who knew my family's dark secrets.

I did well in the Marines. I managed the discipline quite easily, even though I didn't enjoy it. The physical rigors of training didn't bother me in the least, as I was in excellent physical condition. One of the proudest events of my young life was when I was promoted to corporal. I considered my enlistment a positive event in my life, even though at times it was quite frightening and very difficult.

A few weeks after being discharged in 1952, I began a twenty-year career with Mountain Bell Telephone, a subsidiary company of AT&T. I began as a lineman. The work was physically demanding and was just dangerous enough to make it exciting. I loved it.

My rise through the ranks of that huge company was not meteoric, but it certainly could be called exemplary. I was promoted from lineman to combinationman in a small Colorado mountain town. As the title implies, the work included a wide variety of responsibilities: installing and repairing phones, maintaining telephone central office equipment, and maintaining long-distance toll lines in the rugged, mountainous country of central Colorado and a microwave station on top of Monarch Pass. Because of my ability in the mountains, I was also known for a short time by another nickname, "Snowshoe Ham."

During this time I also completed the Dale Carnegie Human Relations Course. In later years I have viewed that experience as pivotal to personal growth and career advancement.

After five years in the mountains I was promoted to salesman and moved my family, a wife and two daughters, to Colorado Springs. After only one year on that assignment I was again promoted, this time to exchange manager in eastern Colorado. About forty men and women reported to me, and again I loved the work.

Three years later, in what I believe was recognition for doing an exemplary job as manager, I was promoted again and moved to the company's headquarters in Denver. My new job was to train other managers in communications, management sciences, and personal growth. It was unusual for someone who didn't have a college degree to receive this assignment. I eagerly read books on psychology, communications, management, motivation, and all other aspects of human behavior. I had found my niche.

The job of management trainer was a rotational, two-year assignment. But instead of rotating back into the regular management ranks of the business after two years, I was selected to become the company's organization development specialist—Mountain Bell's first-ever in-company management consultant.

On this assignment the learning curve was the steepest I had ever encountered. I had no one to look to as a model or mentor. I was often frustrated, but I had a passion for the work, was persistent, and became more competent. I was soon recognized as a useful resource by upper management.

After three years of in-company consulting and after training my own replacement, I was laterally transferred to manage long-distance operators. I enjoyed the assignment, but shortly thereafter I decided to leave the Bell System and pursue my passion of management and communications consulting.

Shortly after leaving the Bell System, I became a consultant to a successful and highly visible orthodontist. Through this man's introduction my insights into management and communications found a ready market in the profession of dentistry. In a very short period of time I became well known within the profession, primarily because of my public speaking ability. I have lectured to dental audiences in almost every state in the United States, in Europe, Canada, and Mexico. I have published a monthly paper on management, communications, and personal and spiritual growth for well over a decade.

In the personal and family dimension of my life, I was married one year after joining the Bell System. The marriage ended in divorce eighteen years later. Two daughters born to the marriage, who were sixteen and thirteen at the time of the divorce, chose to live with me.

I remarried, and my second wife also had two daughters, whom I adopted. At the time of the adoption they were ten and six. Our son was born about two years later. In the eighth year of our marriage we adopted an eighteen-year-old girl who was the best friend of one of our daughters. There has always been an abundance of love in our family. I frequently embarrass my wife, Judy, by saying, "Every day is Christmas."

I have always been an outdoorsman, and as an adjunct to my consulting business for many years I have organized and led wilderness adventure seminars. In this activity I take client friends on horse pack trips, sponsor hunting camps, backpack trips, white water rafting, and float trips down Western rivers. I still enjoy hunting and fishing and I consider myself to be an accomplished fly fisherman.

In my more mature years I believe I have been accepted as one of God's teachers. This book may validate that belief in the minds of those who read it.

*There is within each of us a still
small voice speaking for love. To some it is
the voice of God. To others it is the Holy
Spirit. If there is credit due for this book,
it is to this still small voice it is due.*

— O. A. Bud Ham, April 11, 1995

"WHAT DO I WANT TO COME OF THIS?
WHAT IS THIS BOOK FOR?"

*To help people learn how to reduce or eliminate
fear in their lives by the simple process of
making love-based decisions*

✧

To emphasize that life is choices

✧

*To encourage people to test the usefulness of
applied spirituality*

✧

*To advocate diversity by accepting our
differences in spiritual beliefs*

✧

*To contribute to the spiritual growth of as many
people as possible and thus to their peace
and prosperity*

✧

*To totally accept the first two words of the
Lord's Prayer, which clearly tell us that
regardless of individual life circumstances and
beliefs we are all sisters and brothers,
children of our Father*

✧

*To demonstrate through action steps that peace
and prosperity are available to everyone*

SHARING "MY TRUTH"

My friends tell me I am a good storyteller. If that is so, I am pleased. I assure you that when I lecture, consult, or write, I strive to tell the truth, but it is "my truth." It is the most accurate I can give you at that point in my learning and growth. Perhaps a useful way of helping you understand why "my truth" is in quotes is to read the following story about Truth. I have known the story for many years, and I am sorry I do not know whom to credit for the useful information it contains.

THE OLD LADY IN THE CAVE

Once upon a time there was a man who was in all things successful and comfortable. He had a fine family, money enough to treat his friends, and a craft of which he was justifiably proud. He had an honest name and an untroubled heart, yet still he was not completely happy.

"I must know Truth," he said to his wife.

And because she was wise enough to know that his unhappiness would—in the end—be her own, his wife said to the man, "Then you must seek her until you find her." She packed his bag and sent him out on the road, a beggar after Truth.

The man searched in towns and villages. He looked for Truth in the city streets. He made his way into farmlands, and out to seacoasts, through deserts, and over hilly wastes. After many sleepless nights and tired days, in a small cave near the top of a vast mountain, he found her.

She was not at all what he expected. Truth was a wizened old woman with only a single tooth left in a puckered mouth. Her eyes were rheumy; her skin was drawn and crackled as parchment over prominent bones. Her hair hung in lank, greasy strands on her shoulders. But when she gestured to the man with a hand crabbed with age and called him into the cave, her voice was low and lyrical and pure, and it was thus that he knew that he had found Truth at last.

He spent a year and a day by the old woman's side and learned all that she had to teach. And at the end of that time, he said to her: "My Lady Truth, I left my wife and my family, my hearth and my friends, to be by your side and to learn from you. Now I am ready and must go home. But still, I would do something for you in exchange. What can I do?"

Truth looked at him and cocked her head to one side. She held up an ancient finger. "When you talk of me," she said, "tell them how young and beautiful I am."

YOU ARE IN
THE RIGHT PLACE

*To be happy, successful, healthy,
and prosperous is not complicated.*

✧ ✧ ✧

If you choose to learn and grow toward the quality of life you desire to create, where you are now is *The Right Place.* It cannot be otherwise. You can start from nowhere else. Regardless of your situation—the status of your career, your social life, your family situation, your financial condition, your love life, the health of your body, the health of your mind, the health of your spirit—*you are in the starting gate.* The only questions are: "Will you decide to run?" and "If so, when?"

HOWEVER, do not make the assumption it is easy to become happy, successful, healthy, and prosperous: it is not. It is the unabashed mission of this book to provide you the opportunity, if you are ready, to test the premise of the first sentence in this introduction for yourself. There are innumerable natural and simple truths, any one of which can make your journey through life more peaceful, make you more happy and productive, and thus make the world a better place in which to live.

If you were asked if you seek happiness, you would certainly say yes. Therefore, it is important for you to know in your search for happiness that fear, or any of its derivatives, will rob you of happiness. **You cannot be happy and afraid at the same time!** Whenever your happiness is being blocked by a fear-based thought or emotion you can, **by choice,** select its love-based opposite to recapture your birthright and be happy.

I am referring here to such fear-based derivatives as **selfishness**, which can be replaced with **generosity**; **anger** or **revenge** by **forgiveness**; **despair** by **hope**; and even **prejudice** by **acceptance**.

If you were to say someone made you angry or jealous or sad, isn't it true you would have placed someone else in charge of your quality of life? If you want to be a happier person, it's time you take charge!

You Can Only Be Happy Now

Consider these questions:

◇ At this present moment in time do you have all you really need to be happy?
◇ Do you suppose at this exact time tomorrow the same will be true? How about five years from now?
◇ Can a homeless person with no money be happy?
◇ Can a homeless person find something for which to be grateful?
◇ Can a seriously ill person be happy?
◇ Is happiness a decision?
◇ Is happiness learned?
◇ Are there action steps to becoming a happier person?
◇ Must you earn happiness?

Happiness and Time

You cannot be happy "then," either the "then" in the future, or the "then" of the past. You can think of a past event, which can bring pleasant memories and contribute to your happiness now. Likewise, you can have pleasant thoughts and anticipation about an expected happy event in your future, which can contribute to happiness now. These are appropriate thoughts, but you can only be happy now!

If you are one who chooses to delay happiness until retirement or until the last child is successfully launched, or until your portfolio has reached a certain value, you are delaying your happiness out of existence. Conversely, if your only joy is reliving the events of the past, your joy disappears when you are rudely jerked back to the present reality.

Thieves of Happiness

By far the most common thieves of happiness are pain and fear. To understand these two mentally manufactured impostors is critically important as one charts a path toward a happy "now."

Emotional Pain

Emotional or psychological pain is always pain of the past. Perhaps it is caused by a perceived failure on your part, such as not completing some long ago assignment. Or perhaps you did something that hurt you or someone else. The pain is typically guilt or its close relative, shame. Sometimes the robber is sadness or feelings of inferiority. You can prove to yourself that these thieves of happiness do not exist **except in your mind.**

Fear

This may come as a surprise to you, but fear is **always** fear of the future! The future and the past do not exist, **except in our minds!** Instead of "fear" we sometimes use the words "concerned," "anxious," or "worried." Some of us have been taught that worry is necessary for us to fulfill our responsibilities. Current enlightened teaching helps us know that fear is a controllable and totally unnecessary negative emotion and worry accomplishes nothing!

Is it easy to gain control over fear? Certainly not. We can quite easily visualize a situation in our minds where we may not be able to overcome fear, such as riding in a vehicle totally out of control down a steep mountain pass or looking into the barrel of a robber's gun. **But this does not negate the reality that, if we choose to, we have the ability to displace the vast majority of our fear-based thoughts, and thus cope more effectively and have considerably more happiness!**

No matter what is going on in your life now, you can identify things you would like to have happen that would produce an ideal day for you. There is a simple formula you will be introduced to in this book, which, if you choose to implement, will ensure you of more ideal days.

What if, down deep in your being, you and all of the people in business, schools, health care, factories, government—all people everywhere—committed to live by what is probably the greatest simple truth of all? It is:

Do unto others as you would have them do unto you.

Wouldn't that solve the world's problems and make it a happier place? Just where do we start if we really

want to live in a kinder and gentler world and are
willing to do our part?

There is only one place where you can start—
WITH YOU!

What if you made the commitment to attempt to
live your life according to the Golden Rule, would
you be happier? Would it influence what **you** think
of yourself and what others think of **you**? Would
your family and associates be happier because of
your commitment? Would **you** laugh more? Do you
suppose the quality of **your** life would change?

As I discuss the application of "The Rule," which
has been around for a couple of thousand years, I
occasionally hear references to what some think is a
higher rule—the Platinum Rule—"Do unto others as

they would have you do unto them." The Platinum Rule has one flaw, which I think almost invalidates it. **Only rarely can I be sure how another wants me to treat her or him.** So maybe we would do well to diligently try to live by the original and simpler rule for another thousand years or so!

Building a Philosophical Foundation

It can be said this book is a journey with encouragement for readers to know they can achieve the four goals of happiness, success, health, and prosperity, but in a broader sense it is much more.

It is clear that our world and our brothers and sisters who live in it with us are in trouble. It may be impossible for us to accurately measure whether mankind is in a downward spiral toward becoming a less happy, less successful, less healthy, and less prosperous species, or is making upward progress toward those goals and simply not aware of it. However, very few if any of us would deny there is a great deficiency in the fulfillment of those goals for the vast majority of human beings. The following list of societal deficiencies clearly tells us there is much room for improvement and therefore much work to do.

✧ Countless thousands of children go to bed hungry every night. Many of them are cold and wet.
✧ Children carry guns to school.
✧ We are losing the war on drugs.
✧ Fifty percent of marriages end in divorce, most of them bitter endings.
✧ The costs of ordinary health care are extraordinary. It can cost a young couple one month's combined earnings for one illness of their child, to treat what was once known as a common cold.

✧ There is an outbreak of clergymen sexually molesting children.
✧ The number of unemployed people is huge and is probably surpassed by the number of underemployed.
✧ Some religions are teaching fear, hatred, and separation from others who believe differently.

Clearly something is very wrong. Are there answers? Of course there are! Mankind has been given problems that have simple, clearly understandable solutions. However, finding those solutions that we personally can implement will be greatly facilitated if we have clarified our personal philosophical foundations.

A Philosophical Premise: Life Is a School

Why am I here? What is life about? Do I have a purpose beyond existing day to day? Do I have a mission, or is life just one great accident? These questions have been asked throughout history. If you can accept the idea that life is a school, you may also accept my belief about our primary mission in life: **To learn lessons and become as Godlike as we possibly can while living with our falibility.**

As students in life's school we must understand we cannot avoid being teachers. If you want to learn something, anything, **teach it!** Being a teacher shortens the time interval between receiving useful, new information and the successful application of that information.

All of us have had problems in our lives. The rest of the story is that if you live much longer you will experience many more events that you might categorize as problems. What is it worth to you to **know** every time you have a problem, **any problem**, you can turn it into a positive learning experience and fear it no longer?

The Energy to Change

Yes, change takes energy. Do you tire easily now? If so, it may well be because of all the negative energy in your life. **Negative energy cancels out a like amount of positive energy!**

In this book we will be concerned with three types of energy: physical, mental, and love. To increase any one form of energy increases the other two in your energy pool or reserve. Contrary to what you may have experienced in the past, increasing available energy to do the things that will increase your happiness is not difficult. In fact it will take far less energy to adopt this new way of thinking and being than the energy you are expending now.

You will not only empower yourself, but others. If you undertake this growth process, you will indeed become a positive change model for those closest to you, provided they are ready to take charge of their lives.

You have all the energy you need to begin to progress toward your greater happiness—it is just a matter of using it in ways that have a higher probability of desirable payoff.

Trust-Based Relatioinships

Why are some people able to create instant good vibes with almost everyone they meet? Is it a matter of luck that some people have friendships that last for a lifetime?

There are so few people who understand the dynamics of relationship building that it could be referred to as the best kept secret of interpersonal relationships. What has to happen between two people before mutual respect starts to develop, or that most important of all relationship elements, trust? **Regardless of past interpersonal difficulties, trust can be rebuilt between two people!** You will be introduced to a simple process that becomes easy with practice.

Relationship building is a series of events. Once we understand the dynamics, we can speed up the process and retain a greater number of long-term, mutually satisfying relationships. These relationships might be with friends, customers, patients, or clients **but especially with spouses and family members!**

You will be introduced to "relationship insurance," the only such policy in existence, and it is yours for the taking. All that is required is awareness of how to proceed, a little time, a desire to maintain this more satisfying way of relating, and a willingness to risk minor short-term discomfort for major comfort later.

Using Your Resources to Facilitate Your Journey

According to two recent polls by reputable research firms, 94% of Americans believe in God. It is reasonable to assume that 80% of the believers pray, at least on occasion. Many of those who pray, only pray when they are experiencing painful difficulties in their lives.

I'm not suggesting praying only in time of need or during a crisis is inappropriate. **However, if you believe in God, you will be encouraged to consider using this spiritual resource on a continuous basis.** This applied spirituality is a very practical tool that can help you be more successful, happier, healthier and more prosperous. Perhaps after working through some of the easily understood and implemented tests contained in this book, you will elect to use the resource of prayer on a more continuous basis.

I suggest it is most appropriate for you to test spirituality to see if it will be useful to you. Additionally, there are ways of putting your faith to work of which you may not be aware. **But unless you personally give it a shot you will never know if applied spirituality can help you hit your targets.**

I have written this book with a firm intent to utilize applied spirituality during the writing. It is my desire that this book be maximally beneficial and challenge the thinking of as many people as possible as they proceed on the journey we call life, be they atheist, Buddhist, Christian, Jew, or of any other belief.

This book is greatly influenced by the teachings of Jesus because of the teachings of the culture of my birth. It is my belief that just for the asking He continues to offer us understanding and enlightenment. I believe he also implores us not to separate ourselves from our brothers and sisters whose heritage by birth gives them a different perspective. What is written here is not limited by any church rules, dogma, or doctrine. Contrary to some theology, Jesus does not teach separation. Neither did Buddha or Krishna. **May those who read this book experience an increase in tolerance for those who are different from them—in belief—in race—in culture—in sexuality—and more nearly accept that we are, in truth, all brothers and sisters.**

Each chapter in this book begins with philosophy, principles, and poetry relevant to the content of that chapter. Unless otherwise noted they are written by the author. Please consider the following as clarifications.

Philosophy. My philosophy is mine alone, even though none, or at least very little of it is original. Dale Carnegie said he stole much of his philosophy from Jesus, Plato, and others. I shall be honored if you choose to steal some of mine for yourself.

Principles. *Principles are truths we can depend on, but if defined by man they are not without exception.*

Poetry. *Poetry can only be a gift to another poet. So who is a poet? One who writes poetry? Yes, but aside from writing, a poet is anyone who sees beauty in the world and helps others to see their own beauty and completeness.*

CRIPPLE CREEK SALOON 1887

A little man came in from the street
and the wind was whipping his coat.
The boys at the bar paid him no heed
and went on with their beer and jokes.

He was dusty and tired, he looked all wrung out,
and his boots were worn off at the heels.
His back was straight and his eyes were clear
and he always knew how a man feels.

Big Ted, the barkeep who knows people well,
saw the power when the man smiled,
and his words were soft, but heard by all,
like a Master's voice in the wild.

"I'm new in town and we need a church
and I'm going to need some help."
Big Ted said, "Fine," and passed the hat,
but the stranger just held up his hand.

It's not money I need—it's for souls I plead.
A church doesn't have to be built.
From where you sit just give me the nod—
right where we are we can talk to God.

No one said no, and some of the boys
allowed it would be alright.
He began to speak, and the words were heard
by cowboys and miners alike.

He didn't talk of pain or fear,
or the fires of hell below.
"My friends, be kind to your neighbor.
That's all we need to know."

He said men are judged by what they do,
not looks nor who they are.
And the hardest man there had a lighter heart
when the little man left to follow his star.

Chapter One

FULFILLING THE MISSION BY CHOICE

Personal dignity is determined by our thinking, not by our environment.

✧ ✧ ✧

A personal philosophy of faith allows us to function in life like a strong ship in a major storm, under the guidance of a wise captain.

Meeting the Mission

I HAD BEEN IN THE CABIN for all but a few days of the past seven weeks with only my black Labrador retriever for company. My mission was to write a book. My diversions were a radio that could pick up two country music stations from Helena, an audiotape player, reading, watching wildlife, and playing fetch with my dog.

It was an ideal place for an introspective sabbatical, during which I pursued the activities of thinking, praying, meditating, reading, and writing. I cooked and ate when I was hungry, slept when I was tired (sometimes at mid-day), read when it suited my fancy, and wrote when I felt inspired.

My family and friends had heard me talk of the book I was going to write **someday** for over ten years. Some of them had begun to doubt it would ever be written. It wasn't that they didn't love and respect me, or that they didn't think I had the book in me—but ten years is a long time for just talk and no action.

However, as the demands for my time from my company and my family diminished, my commitment to begin the book intensified. My desire to begin grew

even stronger when I was encouraged by an old friend. My friend had written three books in four years. All had qualified as best-sellers.

Then it happened. The last barrier to taking a writing sabbatical was removed by a fairly recent acquaintance who had great faith in my message. The acquaintance gave me an advance of several thousand dollars, which was enough to meet my income requirements for over a month.

I selected the ideal place for the retreat. It was a snug, well-equipped but isolated hunting cabin in the Madison Range in Montana. I arrived there in mid-February. The snow was deep, even for my four-wheel drive pickup. The last quarter mile was just too steep, and the truck became hopelessly stuck in a deep drift.

For the next two days I trudged back and forth carrying in my books, writing paraphernalia, clothing, personal effects, and my supply of groceries. I also carefully carried in two bottles of eighteen-year-old, single malt Scotch whiskey (a gift from a friend who wished me well) and several well-aged bottles of my favorite Cabernet Sauvignon.

Some of my friends openly expressed their concern about my adjustment to being alone for several weeks with just my dog for company. My close friends and family never doubted my ability to handle the solitude well and were happy I had been given the opportunity.

I organized the work area in the cabin with great excitement. The writing progressed. The hours flew by, and days turned into weeks. The only discipline I held myself to was regularly exercising on my NordicTrack, which I had also laboriously carried from the truck to the cabin.

The flow of words from my mind to my finger tips, thence to the word processor keyboard usually poured out easily, on occasion for hours at a time. When the flow of words dried up, I would take a break and perhaps go snowshoeing, or saw and split wood, which was a daily chore. Sometimes I would read, or clean the cabin, wash the dishes, exercise, or prepare the next meal. Every few days I would trudge through the snow down to my truck and run the engine for a few minutes.

Prayer and meditation were regular activities, sometimes several times a day. But always early and late. Writing the book became the strongest passion I had experienced in my sixty years. On days when the words didn't flow so easily I enjoyed the distraction of watching wildlife, which had always been a major interest. It was like watching my own personal nature channel on television. Deer, elk, coyotes, rabbits, eagles, and ravens passed through my view almost in a continuous flow.

The passion of my mission had its roots in my youth when I rejected the dogma and doctrine of organized religion. I drifted in and out of several Christian denominations, always seeking answers to questions that religious people could not answer to my satisfaction.

My joy and enthusiasm for life and learning have been sharply curtailed by the sobering reality that we live in a troubled world from which I cannot escape. I frequently think of the many children who go to sleep hungry every night, many of them wet and cold. I also think about the many sons and daughters of God who wander homeless, hungry, and confused in every major city.

I am also painfully aware of the horrendous wave of violence sweeping the country, bringing unspeakable pain to victims and perpetrators. I pray for both.

I also pray for the safety of the policemen and police-women who are caught up in the mayhem.

The mission of my writing was to tell people there must be, there had to be, a better way. I believe what we are doing now as a society isn't working and so we must try something different. I am locked in to a mind-set that tells me, **"If what we are doing isn't working, it's just common sense to experiment, test, try something different—but don't continue doing what isn't working!"**

Much of my excitement before leaving on the odyssey came from planning the entire event, thinking through all I might need, putting my truck in excellent mechanical condition, and so on. Prior to the actual preparation for my departure from my family I made lists of all the things I might need or want. I made lists of physical needs—clothes, food, computer, printer, paper, and so forth. I also considered what books, tapes, notes, previous writings, including my poetry, would be useful.

The packing phase finally arrived, and I had packed several boxes of books, binders full of old notes, and other paraphernalia. Just as I was closing the last box, without really knowing why or thinking much about it, I included a book I had never read, which had been given to me several years before. I was indeed well prepared when the departure time finally arrived. With books, clothing, food, exercise equipment, computer, printer, and recording equip-ment, my truck had nearly a full load.

And now, in the cabin, after several hours of writ-ing I found myself staring out the window checking the weather and looking for wildlife. It wasn't stress-ful for me when the words stopped flowing. So, this particular afternoon when the words wouldn't come,

I took a break. After the normal diversions and taking care of some of the chores, I picked up the book I had brought almost as an afterthought. Before I had finished many pages I knew the book, *Joshua*, was a Godsend and would contribute greatly to my mission.

For the next couple of days other diversions and even housekeeping chores were largely ignored. Reading *Joshua* became my diversion, my pleasure, and a passion of its own. I believed it to be one of the most beautiful books I had ever read, and I didn't want it to end. The story was instrumental in causing me to powerfully recommit to the teachings of love at a deep and meaningful level.

After I finished reading the book in late afternoon, I sat quietly for a long time. The fire had burned out, and the cold in the cabin became intolerable as twilight descended. I had spent about two hours in deep thought reformulating how I would strive to live my life henceforth. The cold forced me to return to reality, and I rebuilt the fire.

Somewhere along the way, you too will begin to prepare, with great excitement, for your journey to a barely visible and largely unknown destination. *However, you will have the option of leaving fear behind, and you will know you are going to arrive at the right place, at exactly the right time.*

LIFE IS CHOICES

There are many reasons why
we say we can't and don't.
There are others who are shy
and suffer much from won't.

There are some who say they can and will
and thereby hangs a tale indeed
of good and peace and love and toil
to satisfy a spirit's need.

When God gave us the blessing
of a will that is free,
He also gave us choosing—
winning or losing is up to me.

Chapter Two

HUMANKIND'S PROGRESS OUT OF ANIMALISM

*Who I am cannot be determined by the scientific
method. The reward for long periods of searching to
find out what I am brings increasing periods of
peacefulness—the absence of fear.*

❖ ❖ ❖

*I have been taught that I cannot gain
from another's loss, nor lose from another's gain.
Anything I do to help another helps me.
Anything I do to hurt another hurts me.*

❖ ❖ ❖

*It is as contrary to God's plan for us to be concerned
only for the welfare of others as it is for us to be
concerned only for our own welfare.*

Sorting Out What to Do from What to Be

IF I AM WHAT I DO, I AM INDEED IN TROUBLE! But I am
not what I do—nor what I eat (pardon to the memory of Adele Davis)—nor what I wear (clothes do
NOT make the man)—nor am I what I say (thank
God). ***But I am, or will become, what I think.***

*If I am not for myself, who will be for me;
and if I am only for myself, what am I?*
TALMUD—R. Hillel

Evolution of Understanding
The First Law: The Law of the Jungle

*It was just after midnight. All but the bedroom
lights were on in the small, three-room house. A
dark haired, six-year-old boy opened the bedroom door and rubbing his sleep-clouded eyes
asked, "What's wrong Momma? Why is Daddy
home? What is he going to do with the guns?"*

*The Great Depression died slowly in the small
towns of southern Colorado. The hopelessness
and near helplessness of that difficult time lent
an ugly congruence to the events of that warm
spring night in Florence, Colorado, in 1938.*

*My father, Alonzo F. Ham Jr.—Lon or Lonnie
to his family and friends—was a strange
combination of saint and son-of-a-bitch. This
night he would reinforce either opinion,
depending on what one viewed as appropriate
punishment for a black man, who, it was
rumored, had impregnated a white woman.*

*Lonnie was the all night man at the Florence
Auto Company—Hienie Fox's Ford garage.
Directly across Main Street from the garage
was the Magnet Cafe and Bar. The Magnet
was a favorite hangout of the coal miners,*

especially the younger ones who were all in favor of a bit of hell raising from time to time. The crowd in the saloon was unusually loud, and there was a steady stream of roughly dressed men coming and going.

This evening the sounds from the Magnet were strangely different and seemed to create an electricity. Lonnie's curiosity was about to get the best of him when one of the local good ol' boys came by and filled him in on the happenings in the bar. He said, "Them bastards are crazy, Lon. They're gettin' together a neck tie party for Nigger Bob."

"Hell, it's just liquor talk," Lonnie responded.

"Well, maybe so," his companion theorized, "but you cain't deny somethin's got to be done when a white woman has a pickaninny." For over a week the whole county had been agog over the birth of a black baby to a white woman named Laureen.

The loud guffaws and occasional shouts of "hang the black bastard" were clearly heard by Lonnie as he was leaning against the gas pump. His curiosity got the best of him, and he walked across the street to get a clearer understanding of what was really happening. As he nonchalantly leaned against the open doorway of the saloon, he quickly concluded that the black man, Bob Holloway, was indeed in big trouble.

The black family was a curiosity, the only one in the area. It is unclear when they had moved to the South Field coal mining area in Fremont County, Colorado, about eight miles south of Florence. For some years Bob Holloway had been the night watchman at Jim Perrino's coal mine.

Racial prejudice was strong. If Bob and his family came to town on Saturday, as was their custom, they weren't really welcome anywhere. They were tolerated at Ruger's General Store, but if they wanted something to eat, such as a hamburger, they couldn't just walk into the Silver State Cafe. Someone else had to do that for them, some white person. Often that person was Lonnie.

Lonnie was regarded as a maverick by almost all who knew him. He usually took the opposite or unpopular side of current issues. He was radically opposed to President Franklin Roosevelt's New Deal politics and government welfare programs. He enjoyed the notoriety of being Bob's friend.

Bob, his wife, and four children lived in a small shack about fifty yards from the mine tipple. The small dwelling was covered with rusty, corrugated iron siding. No one else lived within a mile of the mine.

Part of Bob's job was to get up at any hour of the night and sell coal to any customer who had the misfortune to need it badly enough to haul it at night. Usually the customer was driving a pickup truck or pulling a two-wheeled, bumper hitched trailer behind his car. Bob was always smiling and helpful.

It wasn't the least bit disturbing to Bob when he was awakened by the headlights of a car shining through his window. He arose and lit a coal oil lamp.

He was surprised to see the car, which he recognized, being driven off quickly and parked behind the tipple. He became alarmed when Lonnie shouted to him as he ran out of the shadows, wildly waving a shotgun and telling him to get back in the house and blow out the lamp. Black people didn't question white men in the 1930s, especially if the white man had *a gun. Besides, Lonnie had befriended him on a number of occasions, so he did what he was told.*

Lonnie had positioned himself on the front porch and was waiting with fearful anticipation. In a few seconds Bob rejoined him, and before Bob could speak Lonnie said, "Bob, they are comin' to hang you."

The only thing the frightened Bob could say was, "Why?"

"They think you are the father of the black baby that woman Laureen had."

"My God, Lonnie, that ain't my baby. I never touched that woman in my life."

Lonnie said, "I believe you, but they are comin' anyway."

"Who's comin'?" asked Bob.

"A bunch of drunk miners."

"What are we gonna do, Lon?"

Lonnie answered in part by taking a .32 caliber Iver-Johnson revolver from his belt and handing it to Bob. "If I can't stop them, you would be better off bein' tried for self-defense. They really do aim to hang you. I called the sheriff in Canon City, but he wasn't there. Maybe they can find him, and he will come in time."

All Bob could say was, "Lordy, I hope so."

When the sheriff and his deputy finally arrived, they had to park their car up on the main road about fifty yards from the shack. The road to the shack and the mine tipple was blocked with cars and pickup trucks. The two of them were almost running as they approached the tight cluster of men and vehicles immediately in front of the shack. When he heard the shotgun blast the sheriff was sure he was too late to prevent a tragedy.

Many of the cars and trucks had their headlights shining directly on the shack. Just seconds before the sheriff and his deputy had arrived on the scene, terrible epithets and threats were being shouted at Lonnie, "Nigger lover!" and "We'll hang you, too, if we have to!"

Lonnie ducked away from a thrown rock, and it crashed through the window of the shack. He deliberately fired his shotgun into a large galvanized steel washtub that was hanging on the side of the porch. The muzzle blast and the noise of the shot hitting the tub had a momentary sobering effect on the mob and caused them to scatter.

Before they had time to regroup, the sheriff and deputy were in front of them with their revolvers drawn. The sheriff fired his twice in the air to further get their attention. "Go on home boys," he said. "There won't be a hangin' here tonight." Lonnie and the sheriff had pre-

*vented the law of the jungle from being
enforced in the mid-twentieth century.*

As in the story of Lonnie and Bob, there are people yet today who run afoul of society's laws by act-
ing out the law of strength—the law of the jungle.
Certainly lynch mobs or, for that matter, all lawless
mobs are examples.

Some Progress in Understanding

*By the summer of 1977 my eldest daughter,
Peggy, had been living independently for three
years. During that period she had borrowed my
pickup truck—and me—to move three different
times as she upgraded her apartment to coin-
cide with her increased income. Therefore I was
not surprised when she came to my office one
day with a request to help her move again. Only
this time she was moving in with George.
George was several years her senior, a divorced
man with two nearly grown children, very dig-
nified, very tall, and very black. George helped
me overcome my prejudice. He has been one of
my beloved sons-in-law for over thirteen
years.*

The Evolving Growth of Understanding

The **evolution of understanding** implies that
humankind has been on a learning journey designed
to culminate in becoming the loving beings we were
created to be. I subscribe to the idea that if we, as
individuals, prepare ourselves for the next step in our
evolution to higher levels of learning, the opportunity
for increased knowledge and understanding will be
provided. I am convinced this Chinese proverb is

God's promise:
When the student is ready, the teacher will appear.

This same evolutionary law can be accepted as operating for all of humankind. This line of thinking suggests as we grow intellectually and spiritually we continue to prepare ourselves to evolve and become ready for a higher law. The process can be described in the following sequence:

✧ from time immemorial—**The Law of the Jungle** "survival of the fittest or strongest"
✧ from Biblical times, The Old Testament—**The Law of Moses** "an eye for an eye, a tooth for a tooth"
✧ from Biblical times, The New Testament—**The Law of Jesus** "turn the other cheek"
✧ from contemporary times—**The Law of Love** "the abandonment of the fear of God"

Survival of the Strongest

For countless centuries the only law governing the emerging human animal was survival of the fittest—the law of the jungle—or tribal laws that man formulated. In the practice of those laws, the physically stronger person could take any possession of a weaker person, including children, spouse, or even the person's life. The law of the jungle was effectively unchallenged in the Mid-Eastern and Western World until the law of Moses entered the scene. The natural law, survival of the fittest, is still completely governing nature and all living things in the wild.

(*NOTE:* As I write these words, I am approaching the midpoint of a month-long writing sabbatical. It is March 2, 1993. I am securely ensconced in a warm and comfortable log cabin with my faithful companion Bham, my black Labrador retriever. We are at the end of a road in the Madison Range about twenty-five miles south of Ennis, Montana.)

The greatest distraction to my productivity is watching the continuous scenarios played out by the deer, rabbits, eagles, ravens, magpies, elk, and coyotes. This morning as Bham and I began our day, there were thirty-five elk feeding within four hundred yards of the cabin.

The law of the survival of the fittest has been operating, clearly observable, right in front of my eyes. A few days ago during a snowstorm, two mature coyotes pulled down, and eventually killed and ate a yearling deer they were able to separate from the main herd. The law of the jungle was not kind. The small deer died hard.

The Law of Moses

The basic law of Moses can be summed up as "An eye for an eye and a tooth for a tooth." This was a quantum leap from the previous laws governing mankind's interactions with his fellow human beings. It is evident from stories in the Old Testament that the shift was so radical it created many years of lawlessness among those, undoubtedly the stronger, who saw the new law as depriving them of what was formerly their prerogative—what they could take.

The Law Of Jesus

Then along came Jesus with another new

law, which stipulated if we are struck on the cheek we must not strike back or demand retribution. We must turn the other cheek! *What a quantum leap from the law of Moses!*

In fact, it was such an advance that in all societies throughout the world not one has tailored the laws of man to emulate the law Jesus introduced. Yet we have ample evidence that it works. We need only to consider the modality and effectiveness of Martin Luther King Jr. and Mahatma Gandi.

No! They did not perfectly employ the law of love, but they gave us shining examples, in contemporary times, to study as models. The laws of most societies around the world today are patterned almost completely according to the law of Moses and yet, for two thousand years we have known of a higher law.

As I see it, it is important for us to acknowledge which law we are operating under, make choices, and on occasion as individuals bolster our courage and implement the laws of love. **If enough of us do that in our daily lives, seek to continually increase the application of turning the other cheek, in all of our dealings with each other, someday it can indeed be the model for the laws of the societies in which humankind lives.** *Yes, this tells us when we have a grievance against another person our best course of action is forgiveness, not a lawsuit!*

The law of love can influence every facet of our daily lives. It teaches us that when confronted by the beggar on the street we should give according to his need and our ability and not be influenced by **our perception of his level of deserving.** If we adopt Jesus' teaching we will love ourselves and the beggar more if we extend generously, which is merely sharing what is ours only by the gifts and grace of God. Jesus admonishes us to be great givers. He further tells us that when we experience lack and our supply channel seems to be blocked, the way to open it again is to give something away!

If humankind is to advance, our laws must advance. This advance can only begin with the thinking of individuals—you and me—training ourselves by visualizing opportunities wherein we have the option to turn the other cheek. **And if a man asks us for our shirt, give him our coat also.**

Let us not become discouraged because progress seems to be so slow. To us a normal life represents a long time—more than seventy years. But in God's reference there is no time, just eternity. The two thousand years since the resurrection of Jesus is but a blink of God's eye!

Growing Past Fear: Recent Revelations

In recent years there have been numerous books and articles published on what are referred to as "life after death experiences" or perhaps more accurately as "near-death experiences." In the typical scenario individuals have been pronounced as physically dead and have somehow come back to life. If this has been going on for centuries, it was not commonly reported and recorded. Rather, it would seem, it is a fairly recent phenomenon.

It has been reported by so many rational, respected persons of integrity that it is very difficult to ignore, provided, of course, one has an open mind. There are so many similarities in the stories they are beyond randomness, and the sources of the reports are so widespread collusion would be next to impossible.

Perhaps the most significant, consistent result for

those who have had the experience is that, as they looked down upon their lifeless bodies, without exception, each said they felt a complete sense of safety and love—so complete they no longer fear death!

Isn't it possible these are contemporary revelations, **miracles,** for the further enlightenment of God's children?

A Philosophy of Death

To have an adequate philosophy of life, one must also have a philosophy to guide him or her through that certain journey we refer to as death. That transformation is a manifest destiny, for ourselves, for all of our loved ones and, of course, for all living things to fulfill.

A well-thought-out personal philosophy on this subject will enable us to cope more maturely with our own transformation when our time comes. If we happen to be one who is blessed with many years of life on earth we will surely experience the passing of many loved ones. To possess such a philosophy will enable us to deal more maturely with our own sense of loss during such times and give us the strength to do God's work by helping others during their bereavement.

If you do not have a personal philosophy that will aid you in the transformation of crossing over, perhaps the following will help:

We are born unequal.
✧ *some with beautiful, strong, healthy bodies and minds and some with lesser*
✧ *some in beautiful places to live, some in ugly ghettos*
✧ *some into wealth, some into poverty*

We live unequally.

✧ *some live many years, some only a short time*

✧ *some with many material possessions, some with virtually none*

✧ *some seem to accomplish much, some seem to accomplish little*

✧ *some would describe their lives as happy, some as unhappy*

✧ *some die easily without pain, some die hard with great pain*

Perhaps death is the only equal event in our lives.

✧ *our physical body is left behind, pain filled or painless*

✧ *even the wealthiest leaves this life without a possession*

*In truth, we are unequal only by man's inadequate ability to measure. God has no special relationships. We must understand that His love extends equally to every one of His children, even though we do not have the same assets and liabilities and are not given (and do not need) the same learning experiences in life. God leaves nothing to chance. **There is no such thing as an untimely death.***

Philosophers and spiritual teachers have told us for centuries that one cannot fully live until one is no longer afraid to die. Many, whom we otherwise would consider as strong and mature, refuse to think about or discuss their own physical mortality. As a result countless people experience the agony of great fearfulness when their passing is imminent.

Our Part in God's Plan

It is apparent to any who care to look that we have much work to do and every person is part of the project! If we are actually afraid of death, as by far the majority of people are, we are weakened, many almost to the point of being immobilized, because of the fear of that unavoidable event in our lives. The opportunities to do God's work are on every hand, **available to every one of us every day!** *Life is choices—life is simple—but it is not easy!* If we are weak or immobilized by fear, we cannot fulfill our part in God's plan to save ourselves. Nor can we effectively help others with their learning and their struggles.

The fear of death is, of course, the fear of God and that He may not keep His promise of love. It was the teaching of the fear of God that contributed to my drifting away from the fundamentalist religion into which I was born. As early as nine years old, I asked one of my grandfathers, "Grandpa, why should I be afraid of God if He loves me so much?"

His response was, as accurately as I can remember it, "Son, you needn't be afraid of God, just His wrath." That didn't make sense to me, and when I questioned further I was told I must accept some things on faith.

My grandfather was the fill-in minister of our small Baptist Church. When the regular minister was away Grandpa Ham would deliver the sermon. I was very proud when he did.

Grandfather gave me many wonderful spiritual gifts. He was a great model of honesty and integrity as evidenced in the following story:

> *On a snowy day, when I was about nine years old, I rode with Grandpa as he drove to the general store for needed supplies. The storm*

had intensified into a fierce blizzard by the time we left the store. We were over halfway home when, without explanation, Grandpa pulled the car off to the side of the road and extracted the contents from a pocket of his overalls. He carefully counted the coins, and I heard him comment, "Just as I thought."

Much to my concern because of the storm, he turned the car around and we went back to the store. We arrived just as the owner was pulling down the shade on the door and closing the store because of the blizzard. Grandpa didn't go into the store. He just handed the owner the amount he had been undercharged for the purchases.

I want to believe that my grandfather performed such noble acts because of love, **but because he feared God's wrath it is entirely possible he did so because of fear.**

It is my contention that the near-death experiences mentioned earlier are contemporary miracles. Isn't it possible they were given to us to help usher in another era in mankind's growth toward oneness with God, by His plan, an era wherein we do God's work because of love, not fear? Let me encourage you to carefully think through the following:

There is no right reason to do a wrong thing. However, there can be a wrong reason to do a right thing. **But the action is infinitely easier to perform and has promise of producing greater results, if we do the right thing for the right reason.**

To do a loving act because of fear demeans the loving act.

Continuity of Revelations

Questions to Ponder

✧ Isn't it possible God is still trying to increase the enlightenment of all of his children?

✧ Did God stop trying to inform his Christian children after John Wycliffe's translation of the Latin Vulgate Bible into English in the fourteenth century?

✧ Do you believe Moses performed miracles?

✧ Do you believe Jesus performed miracles?

✧ Do you believe the founders of the other great religions of the world performed miracles?

✧ Do you believe Billy Graham, Oral Roberts, Joseph Smith, or Norman Vincent Peale have performed miracles?

✧ Do you believe you can perform miracles?

✧ If you are a Christian, do you recall Jesus saying you could perform miracles?

New Age: What Does It Mean?

Obviously those two words can take on any meaning you want them to. For some people these words cause fear. For others the words cause elation and joy and the promise of greater understanding of the God within—the Holy Spirit and brotherhood and the hope of a kinder and gentler world.

Many times in his or her life every spiritual person has come to the realization, **"God works in mysterious ways his miracles to perform."** Many fundamentalist Christians have found the Bible to be the only written resource they need. Many other believers in God and Jesus have found supplemental writings to be of tremendous value. Is one group wrong and the other right when both are trying to live according to the teachings of Jesus?

Additionally, there is much Christians can learn from Buddhists, Hindus, Muslims, and Jews, and likewise members of those religions can learn from Christianity. **"New age" can mean an age in which all faiths can accept each other as children of God—as true brothers and sisters of our one Creator. Let us keep in mind the first two words of the Lord's Prayer are "Our Father," not "My Father."**

If we are released from fear by placing all of our faith in God, we have acquired freedom that can facilitate spiritual growth. We can even read something considered oppositional to our frame of religious reference and perhaps be introduced to a useful idea or a clarification for the first time.

> *Without fear and with faith in a Greater Power, we can always sort out what is wheat and what is chaff in terms of its usefulness to our own spiritual growth.*

Do Something Different

Let me share with you again a principle we cannot afford to ignore—**"When what you are doing isn't working, it is time to *do something different.*"**

- ✧ It is sad but true, wife batterers were taught brutality in their infancy and formative years.
- ✧ Invariably, parents who physically or psychologically abuse their children were taught abuse by their parents.

✧ There is an abnormally high incidence of alcoholics who have alcoholic parents.

Our growth to higher levels of spirituality demands that we work to better our world by breaking the cycle of such abhorrent behavior. In many cases a spiritually oriented psychotherapist can be a valuable facilitator.

I suggest a person needing this therapy is significantly better off with a spiritually oriented therapist because intelligence without love can be cruel and will usually do more harm than good. It is also true, however, that love without intelligence can be destructive. (Consider the spoiled child.) **Wisdom, which is the hallmark of Jesus' teaching, is the perfect blending of intelligence and love.**

By using spiritual resources, with or without the help of a therapist, anyone who chooses can break any destructive behavior cycle. Is it easy? No! Is it complicated? No, it is simple. But to accomplish change we must close our mind's door to what we know isn't working or is destructive and try something else. If we ask for guidance and if we will listen we can shorten the search for what will work.

Whether one believes in Jesus or not, **no one in his right mind can deny the world would be an infinitely better place to live if all people attempted to live according to His teachings of love, giving up judgment, and attempting to live by the Golden Rule.**

If Christian and non-Christian believers truly seek God's guidance and have faith in His promises, it matters not at all what labels (such as "New Ager") others put on them.

Introduction to *A Course in Miracles*

The three volumes of *A Course in Miracles (Text, Workbook,* and *Manual for Teachers)* were given to me in 1983 by a homosexual acquaintance who wanted to be my friend. My prejudices (fears) at the time only allowed me to be nice to him. These fears may have contributed to my delay in starting the *Course.*

From time to time over the next two or three years I attempted to read in the Text or the Workbook. I had not yet returned to a personal relationship with Jesus at that time and each time I attempted to get into one of the books, it seemed too "Christy" for me.

One day, wanting something to read while riding my exercise bike, I picked up the smallest of the three books—the *Manual for Teachers.* Before I had finished reading "Tolerance" on page eleven, I knew I was going to benefit from the *Course.* I could not possibly have known at that time it would become a life-altering study that has enabled me to live with far less fear and more love, joy, and peace than I ever imagined possible.

A Course in Miracles, on its own pages, suggests it is not for everyone. For the first two years of studying it, I found it difficult to describe to others. Then one morning as I walked into my office I found a book lying face down on the floor in front of the bookshelves. I picked the book up and was starting to return it to the shelf when I absentmindedly thumbed through it.

I quickly recognized the book. It had been sent to me by a client friend several years earlier, but I had not read it. It was *Journey Without Distance* by Bill Skutch. Very quickly I recognized it was describing how *A Course in Miracles* came into being. I became completely fascinated by the book, and I read it in a matter of a few hours. I now refer everyone who is interested to this book.

A Contemporary Miracle

About five years ago I conducted a series of communication and team building workshops in Ft. Myers, Florida. My host for each of these meetings has become a close friend and is a young man who is greatly interested in spirituality. During each of the two-day workshops, he and I would have lunch. The workshops were several months apart and invariably he would ask me, "Bud, what have you been studying lately?"

We usually spent some time talking about *A Course in Miracles*, which we were both studying. Additionally, during one of our luncheons, I told him about a workshop I had attended a couple of months earlier conducted by Emmett Miller, a San Francisco area physician, who no longer practices traditional medicine. Emmett has had great success helping people with guided imagery and other forms of hypnotherapy. I also told him about a book given me by a friend who is a mutual acquaintance. The book, *Original Blessing,* was written by Matthew Fox, a rebel Roman Catholic priest. I found his views very refreshing. Fox teaches we are not born in sin; we are born sinless.

Six months later, my young friend and I were seated at the same restaurant for lunch. He began our conversation by saying with great feeling, "Bud, I can never thank you enough for introducing me to the writing of Emmett Fox!"

I responded that I didn't know what he was talking about and I had never heard of Emmett Fox. He said, "Yes, you have! How can you say that? We sat in this very same booth six months ago, and you convinced me I should read everything Emmett Fox had written."

I explained that I had talked about Emmett Miller and Matthew Fox. He then told me that immediately after the last workshop he went to a bookstore and

asked the clerk to help him find books by Emmett
Fox. The clerk told him there weren't many calls for
Fox's books, but he had a boxed, five-book series;
A Treasury of Emmett Fox.

My friend said, "You are going to love one of
these books, and I brought a copy to give you."
Whereupon he presented me with a copy of Emmett
Fox's interpretation of Jesus' *Sermon on the Mount.*
I must give you a bit more of my personal history to
help clarify the importance of this event.

Travels of a Troubled Spirit

When I was a teenager, I decided to leave the
Baptist Church and become a Methodist. I tried to convince my grandfather, who was the family spiritual
leader, I was changing churches to broaden my understanding of spiritual truth. But the real truth is more
young people attended the Methodist Church. Wouldn't
you know it? There was a girl I was especially interested in who invited me to that church. My relationship
with the girl didn't last long, but I remained a
Methodist for several years.

At a deeper level I know I was seeking answers
to a major question that had concerned me from the
time I was twelve years old. For what seemed a very
long period of time I asked God almost daily, "Why is
Danny crippled, and why am I healthy?" Every night
I asked God to take the strength of one of my arms
and one of my legs and give it to Dan and there
would be enough strength for both of us.

Dan is my only brother, the fifth of our parents'
six children. I was number two in birth order. Dan
and I have four wonderful sisters. It wasn't long after
Danny's birth in March 1944, that it was discovered he
wasn't "normal." He couldn't suckle, he never cried,

and his movements were described as spastic. It was some years before we heard the words "cerebral palsy." I also asked my grandfather, "Why am I healthy and why is Danny crippled?" (I know the acceptable term today is "physically disabled," but in the mid-1940s the term was "crippled.") Grandfather responded by saying, "It's God's will." I could accept that, but, "Why?" Grandfather's fundamentalist understanding and teaching could only allow him to answer, "Buddy, we must take it on faith." I still wanted to know why.

Perhaps the most traumatic thing for me at the time was the recollection of a sermon preached in our church some time before Dan was born. The scripture from which the sermon was taken is, "The sins of the fathers shall be visited on the heads of the sons." I cannot remember the minister's elaboration on the subject. However, when Dan was born with serious physical inadequacies, all I could think of was that our family must have done something terrible to displease God so severely.

Until that time I had always been proud of our family. Now Dan was suffering for "the sins of our fathers." I clearly remember I did not want to talk to anyone about my brother's condition, and I sank deeper and deeper into the conclusion that ours was not a good family.

A few years later, as I was leaving the Methodist Church to become a Presbyterian, one of Grandpa's greatest gift lessons came back to me in sharp focus. In several conversations, without ever using the exact words, he clearly told me it was all right to challenge, to ask questions, and seek answers to anything he, the Bible, or anyone else ever told me.

Later in this book I shall try to help you understand how I arrived at my conviction, many years later, that I have never been in the wrong place. *I was not in the wrong place then. The questions raised by the pain of my brother's disability have been a primary motivation for my spiritual quest during my entire life.* Also, without my grandfather's permission to challenge, which was not typical of his religion, I don't believe I would be writing this book. The things that interest me, what I believe, and what I know would be very different.

Religious Quandaries

I remained a Presbyterian for several years. My first wife and I were married in the church, and I was fairly active until I had a no-win argument with a young and very popular minister about evolution. (To my satisfaction, I **knew** there was a three-toed horse.)

Shortly thereafter I met a friend, who had forsaken the Presbyterian Church to become an Episcopalian. He introduced me to Father Eric, the venerable priest of the local Episcopal Church in Salida, Colorado. Father Eric said he had no problem whatsoever with belief in evolution. After a cursory introduction to Episcopalian philosophy and church history and structure, my wife and I became members of the parish.

I was quite active in the church for the next ten years. I became involved in church politics, serving as a vestryman, junior warden, senior warden, and layreader. For me the increased open-mindedness of the church was a refreshing freedom. It was even acceptable among my contemporaries in the church to read about the life of Edgar Cayce, known as "the sleeping prophet of Virginia Beach."

Exploring the Fringe

A copy of the book *Many Mansions*, a biography of Cayce by Gina Cerminina, was passed around. This happened about the same time (late 1950s) as the publication of Morey Brenstein's book, *The Search for Bridey Murphy.* After I recovered from my initial rejection of the idea, these two books stimulated much thought and discussion about reincarnation. For the next several years this was an exciting exploration for me and led me to an interest in other religions. I purchased and intently studied the book, *Great Religions by Which Men Live.* It was then I had the heretical notion that maybe Jesus wasn't the only son of God. That thought was initially quite troubling, but very fascinating.

I discovered it was a matter of historical fact that some of the Eastern religions have a set of commandments that are so close to those given in the Old Testament, that they must have the same source. Their commandments were given to them many years before they were presented by God to Moses. This awareness didn't cause me to doubt the authenticity of the Judeo-Christian ten commandments— then or now—but it did make it very plain to me that there were other paths besides Christianity from which to pursue oneness with God. For a time this was immensely upsetting. The idea was contrary to everything I had been taught up until that time.

During this same time my career with the Bell Telephone System was advancing nicely. I had several promotions and was enjoying the much-sought-after assignment of management development trainer, in the company's headquarters in Denver. That assignment required me to read books about human behavior on the topics of communication, management, motivation, psychology, personal growth, and the human potential movement. I found the studies intensely interesting, and I loved the role of being a facilitator. (We didn't like the label "teacher.") My pursuit of knowledge of religions was set aside, though I did continue regular church attendance for a time.

Then on one very important Sunday, as the congregation of St. Joseph's Episcopal Church was standing to recite either the Nicene Creed or the Apostle's Creed (I can never remember which), I sat down. The priest, my wife, and several of the other parishioners thought perhaps I was ill. I was not. I could no longer stand and say I believed Jesus was the only son of God.

I explained this to the priest, who was also a friend, and this led to several visits to my home by him and several of the other leaders of the church who diligently but unsuccessfully tried to convince me to change my mind. That was in 1967. Shortly thereafter I announced to my family and close friends that I was an agnostic. It wasn't long until I would tell anyone I was an atheist. My recollection of that decision was a wonderful feeling of freedom, such as one feels after shedding a heavy load.

I learned the atheist's arguments well, such as, "Where was God during the Holocaust?" "Why does He kill babies?" "Well, He allows them to die doesn't He?"

Not infrequently, after such an exchange my old friends would say, "Bud, I'm going to pray for you."

My flippant response was, "I need all the help I can get—ha, ha!"

It wasn't long, however, until I started having some of the same concerns about my new atheist friends that I had had for many years about my Christian and Jewish friends. The atheists didn't ask questions either! They read, discussed, and questioned only in ways that would support their atheistic mind-set. Just as my Christian and Jewish friends did not seek to understand each other or to understand their Buddhist, or Hindu brothers, my atheist friends did not seek to understand spirituality and religion.

One of my greatest difficulties with many organized religions is they teach separation, by default if not intentionally. For example, few Protestants, Catholics, and Mormons seek to understand each other's practice of Christianity, let alone anyone with a different spiritual heritage.

(*NOTE:* There is, however, reason to be optimistic. Vatican II did mark a milestone in the Roman Catholic Church as it sought to begin a healing of the body of Christ—the church. They changed the first letter of Catholic to a lower case "c" to include the whole community of believers!)

As an atheist I enjoyed my hiatus from the weight of religious dogma, but thanks to my grandfather I continued to ask questions and tried to keep an open mind.

During this period I conducted a series of personal growth workshops for Denver Free University. During one of the sessions I was asked by a group of young hippies to join them at a Sunday evening service at a local Spiritualist Church. I agreed, and arrived at the church at the appointed time on the following Sunday evening. My hippie friends never showed up.

Atheism to Spiritualism

That inauspicious visit to a small church with a very different form of worshiping God marked the beginning of my journey out of atheism and back to spiritual study. I shall always be grateful for that reintroduction, and I have deep respect for the religious practices of churches of the National Spiritualist Association of Churches. The foundation of their teaching is love and tolerance. Any minister, priest, rabbi, or other religious teacher was welcome to speak at the church I attended, provided there was a reciprocal agreement.

Many religions have included the belief of Guardian Angels in their teaching. The Spiritualist Churches **really, really** believe in Guardian Angels— spirit guides assigned by God—or Jesus, or the Holy Spirit if you are a Christian. Their teaching is that the task of our spirit guides is to help us as we go through life. It is very comforting to believe we are so attended, and I thank God for those who help me.

The minister of the Spiritualist Church usually presented the lectures. It was explained to me that people attend these services to learn and therefore the minister does not preach to them about what they should or ought to do. The ministers are also practicing mediums and psychic readings are a regular part of their worship service. It was a psychic reading on that first visit that assured my return for more demonstrations of extrasensory perception and spiritual exploration of such things as clairvoyance and clairaudience. Although it is not part of the teaching of the Spiritualist Church, it is clear most members believe in reincarnation.

The events leading up to the psychic reading that piqued my interest occurred as follows: After a fairly typical service, such as one might expect in many Protestant Churches, the minister asked several men and women in the congregation, by name, if they would like to participate in the psychic reading portion of the service. Three or four accepted and some declined. I learned later these people were trained psychics or mediums.

I was fascinated by the messages the mediums directed to various individuals in the congregation of about thirty or forty people. Almost half of the congregation received readings. The messages were almost invariably from a loved one who had "crossed over," their term for death. It was apparent that the medium usually did not know the recipient of the reading. Often the messages were to caution the recipient about a health problem, that some problem they were dealing with would soon be resolved, or to be on the lookout for some hazard or another.

The old minister, probably in his eighties, was the last to stand and give readings. After delivering one or two, he said, "I would like to come to the young man in the last row in the brown leather jacket."

I acknowledged his attention by saying, "Good evening." (That seemed to be the response given by most of those who I thought might be regulars.)

He continued by saying, "I am in touch with a grandfatherly figure. He's a portly man, has a full head of grey hair, wears a mustache and glasses. He says for me to tell you, 'It is important for you to make up your own gosh-darn mind about religion.' That's what he says."

He then focused his attention on another recipient and commenced giving her a reading. I could not doubt the sincerity of the message. He described my grandfather accurately and the message was expressed exactly as Grandfather would have said it. For the next three years I was a regular attendee. During this time I saw many demonstrations of what can only be described as extra psychic phenomenon.

For example, one Sunday evening upon entering the church each member of the congregation was presented with a three-by-five inch card and a short pencil. That evening the church was being visited by an itinerant Spiritualist minister who would deliver the lecture and conduct a psychic demonstration.

Following the lecture the congregation was instructed to write the names of two loved ones who had crossed over and one question on the card. Then we were to fold the card with the message inside the fold.

On my card I wrote the names of Grandfather Ham and Joe Stovall. I had served with Joe in the United States Marine Corps. He was a splendid example of young manhood. He was killed in Korea. My question was, "Should I join the real estate company or the small corporation?" (At this point in my career I had planned to leave the Bell System and had two options: to join a small sales consulting firm as a management consultant or a real estate company, both owned by friends.)

The instructions to the individuals in the congregation were to respond to the psychic if you thought he was addressing you or your question.

While the cards were being collected the visiting minister sat facing the congregation with a folding table in front of him. He was carefully and, to my satisfaction, completely blindfolded. Then the folded cards were deposited in front of him on the table. The psychic then began picking up the cards and discussing his impressions. Various members of the congregation responded.

He had gone through about twenty cards when he picked up a card and said, "I'm in touch with two hams. I see a big ham and a small one. Wait a second—no, I'm in touch with an old ham and a young ham. I also see a stove. Does that ring a bell with anyone?"

I responded by saying, "I'm sure you are talking to me."

He said, "Good. The answer to your question is: by all means join the small corporation."

With that he picked up another card in which I had no interest!

I was impressed. The next day I told my friend in the real estate company I would not be joining him (even though I had completed real estate school and was licensed), and thus began my career as a consultant, which has spanned over twenty years.

I may never know what prompted the minister to ask me, one Sunday evening, to deliver the lecture on the following Sunday evening. I do not know how he knew I was a public speaker. I decided to present "Life Is Choices: Accepting problems as stepping stones to growth or as millstones around our necks is a choice." The lecture, which I diligently held to fifteen minutes, was well received, and I became a frequent speaker.

On several occasions the minister asked me if I would like to join him and the other mediums on the platform to give readings. I had attended several evening training sessions at the church, but I did not consider myself even remotely qualified to give anyone a reading. I always politely declined. Then one evening when he asked me, I surprised myself by accepting. I had no idea what I was going to say, or how it was going to turn out, or even if I would say anything.

I gave two readings that evening. Both were well received. One of them was very specific, and I remember it clearly. I too, spoke to a man in the back row. He was wearing a blue suit. I told him, "You are not to fire the man you are planning to dismiss tomorrow. Rather, it is important for you to clearly explain your expectations to him."

After the service the man thanked me profusely. I had never met him before and have not seen him since. I did not give readings again.

Spiritual Study on Hold

With the energy demands of a new marriage and a new career, I put all spiritual study on a lower priority. I did not stop spiritual study and daily contact with God altogether, but it certainly slowed down. Since that time only rarely have I visited the Spiritualist Church. My spiritual study has taken me in a different direction. I now believe I am guided and directed, or told, what I need to know when I need to know it by my spiritual resources. Yet, I shall always be appreciative of their contribution to getting me back on a spiritual path.

During the succeeding years, at any one time, I was almost always reading spiritually oriented books. I am quite sure many people would label much of this reading material "New Age." As mentioned earlier it is unfortunate these two words raise fear-based rejection among many Christians who otherwise might benefit from a message that is not contained in the Bible.

Coming out of the Closet: Phase One

In early January 1984, I presented a one-day lecture to the District Dental Society in Wausau, Wisconsin. My presentations are always behaviorally oriented. During this lecture I spoke on such topics as leadership, positive mental attitude, management communications, employee motivation, relationship building, and personal and professional integrity.

I enjoyed the lunch break with several dentists, some of whom had heard me lecture before. They were complimentary about the morning session, but for me there seemed to be something missing—there was no intensity, no pizzazz, no passion. I excused myself from the table shortly after the main course was eaten, on the pretense that I didn't want to be tempted by dessert. The real reason I left the table early was I wanted a few minutes alone to think about the afternoon.

I know I was not alone during those few minutes that were available for me to recenter my thinking. It was totally clear to me, as I again approached the podium, that the missing element had been my avoidance of any words relating to spirituality. I had long been in the habit of asking God for his assistance before every lecture. But I had the idea I might displease someone if I dealt with any topic or reference that was not secular.

My commitment, before I again mounted the platform, was to no longer avoid spiritual references in my presentations if I thought they would be helpful, regardless of how some of the audience might feel about my message. Following the lecture both the audience and I were immensely pleased with the afternoon presentation. The spiritual element has been a major part of all of my presentations since that important turning point.

Coming out of the Closet: Phase Two

I had always known, since placing my spiritual growth on a back burner, there would come a time when it would again become my major focus. Even though I openly added spiritual references to my personal speaking presentations, I continued to largely avoid such references in my writing.

During the late summer of 1987 I lectured to a sophisticated dental audience in Banff, Alberta, Canada. Several people came to me after the presentation and expressed their appreciation, especially for the spiritual references. It was then I knew it was time for me to begin the countdown to integrating spirituality into my writing.

At that time I had been writing a newsletter for dentistry, for six years. The paper had always been heavily influenced by my continuing study in management and behavioral sciences, which have little if any reference to spiritual matters. The following announcement was on the front page in the first issue of the seventh year of publication, November 1987:

> *For those who have been long-term subscribers, I shall take this opportunity to thank you for your encouragement, your support, and your patience with my mind wanderings.*
>
> *Firstly, in addressing the changes, I should like to talk more specifically about a change that began rather subtly, and was at first, part of my lecture presentations only. It happened while lecturing to the Wausau Dental Society in Wausau, Wisconsin, in January 1984. It was then I decided to begin sharing more of my thoughts on the spiritual aspects of dentistry.*
>
> *I have now concluded that ignoring the spiritual side of learning has been the missing element in our search for growth. You may have noticed increasing reference to that element in recent issues of this paper. I do not in any way wish to meddle with anyone's religious convictions. I shall however endeavor to use my resources to the fullest to contribute to your spirituality.*

Reconnecting with Jesus

And now after this circuitous lengthy explanation of my spiritual travels, let us return to the importance of my young friend in Ft. Myers miraculously presenting me with Emmett Fox's book, *Sermon on the Mount*.

From the time I left the Episcopal Church in 1967 until reading Fox's book in 1988, I had essentially excluded Jesus from my study, prayers, meditations, writings, and lectures. Perhaps I was afraid Jesus might distance me from my Jewish friends and clients. Perhaps it was because I did not believe then, nor do I believe now, He is the only son of God. (There is a complete elaboration of this position later. Briefly, Jesus is my brother, and we are both sons of God. He got it right, He's the only one who has. The rest of us still have lessons to learn.)

I know, during those years, I only used His name in vain. Emmett Fox's book led me back to a comfortable communication with Jesus. I now believe His "Sermon on the Mount" is the most important series of speeches ever delivered to humankind.

Somehow, until recently, I was ashamed of letting my highly educated and worldly successful friends know I pray on a regular basis. It has only been since I began actively writing this book and the alone time at Finger Mountain Cabin, that I am comfortable telling others I talk to Jesus frequently during my waking hours. And now, in the vernacular of the times, I am tempted to say, "I couldn't care less what others think!" But that's not true. I really do care—more than ever before, **but I am learning to ignore without judgment anyone who chooses to write me off as an extremist, a wacko, or a Jesus Freak.**

The combination of the position of Jesus in *A Course in Miracles*, asserting that each of us, along with Him, is a Son or Daughter of God, and studying *The Sermon on the Mount* has provided a deeper, more intimate relationship and communication with my Chief Spiritual Resource than I ever thought possible.

(*An Aside:* In the last few minutes, as the day draws to a close March 9, 1993, in this isolated Montana hunting cabin where I have come to write, one thing has become abundantly clear to me. The reason for me being here is to pave the way and make it easier—for as many as people as possible who read these words to choose to become one of God's teachers.)

Another Source

Several years ago I was introduced to another book that has also had tremendous impact on my communication with Jesus. Thus, it has greatly influenced how I think and how I live my life. I cannot overstate its value to me.

I was visiting a much loved and very spiritual Roman Catholic friend in Baton Rouge, Louisiana. My friend had invited me to go bass fishing. He approached me in his home the evening before the fishing excursion with a book in his hand and said, "Bud, God told me to give this book to you."

When my friend, whose spirituality I do not question, made the offer, I solemnly and gratefully accepted the gift. It has been my daily companion since. The book is *God Calling*, edited by A. J. Russell. It is readily available. I highly recommend it. Be sure and read the introduction.

At the time I received the gift, I was unaware that I was entering into a period of significant turmoil in my life. The daily lessons in the book, dictated by Jesus to two elderly women in England in the 1930s, has indeed been a Godsend and given me great comfort. There are many parallels between *God Calling* and *A Course in Miracles*. Both were dictated by Jesus, and both focus heavily on ridding ourselves of fear by loving and trusting God.

No matter what seemingly awful thing we expect to happen in our lives, as fear starts to dominate our thinking these books provide clear direction. To regain peace, we must only accept Jesus' teaching and as frequently as needed remind ourselves of His message:

"All is well. Have no fear. I am with you."

There are many useful, beautiful messages in *God Calling*, one for each day of the year, such as the following:

✧ "Work, work, work, and ceaseless activity are not part of our Father's plan."
✧ "Leave planning to me. I am the Architect— you are the builder."
✧ "Never let yourselves think, 'We cannot afford this,' or 'We shall never be able to do that.' Say, 'The supply for it is not here yet, but it will come if we should have it. It *will* surely come."

For daily usefulness I believe the book *God Calling* is without equal.

VENTURING

I've wandered far from my usual tract,
and I've seen the lions' den.
To see it there in truth's bright light
makes it easy to look again.

The fears I had of what it was
lay buried deep inside.
They sought to control my every thought
and strike me terrified.

I'll never go back to where I was,
fearful of what I'd see.
It's clearer now. I have strength to love.
This is how it was meant to be.

Chapter Three

BUILDING TRUST AND LOVE-BASED RELATIONSHIPS

*The natural tendency of humans is to trust.
If we are nontrusting, it is the result of choices
we have made about how we think about some
of life's learning experiences.*

✧ ✧ ✧

*Love is, without exception, the most powerful
and readily available tool we can use to accomplish
our objectives. Fear is love's opposite and the only
reason love is underutilized.*

✧ ✧ ✧

*The way to build relationships, faith, happiness,
and so on, is not to tear down anything anyone
else is building.*

Mentor

HE WAS EIGHTY-SOMETHING *when I was nine.
He was straight, tall, and slim. He was a
neighbor, and I had called him Uncle Bert for
as long as I could remember. To the adults in
the neighborhood he was "Monty"—Albert
Montgomery.*

He was a retired building contractor. After the economic crash of 1929, because there were no buildings to be built, he sold or gave away most of his equipment. In retirement he pursued his hobbies of hunting, fishing, woodworking, and gardening.

Any time a neighbor had a building project such as a coal house, a barn, or adding a bedroom, he would stroll by the site and study it carefully. He never offered his opinions unless asked.

From the time I was a small boy, he always had time for me. He would often tell me stories of his boyhood on a farm in eastern Kansas stories such as shooting waterfowl with a muzzle-loading shotgun. His mother was widowed when he was a small boy. He told me how he contributed financially to the family by trapping muskrats, skunks, and minks. He also told me fishing stories and how great trout fishing was in Colorado in the 1920s.

One hot August afternoon, shortly before my twelfth birthday, he walked into our backyard where my father and I were repairing the pump platform that covered our well. After the usual pleasantries and comments about the heat, he turned to me and said, "Bud, it's time you started trapping. There is an over-population of muskrats and skunks, and it's time you learned how to catch them. I will teach you. Save your money, and buy a dozen Victor traps from the Montgomery Ward catalogue. They will cost you four dollars and fifty cents, plus postage."

I was so excited I found it difficult to sleep nights. In the weeks to come I picked beans, cleaned neighbors' chicken houses, and performed every job I could find to accumulate the money for the traps. I shall never forget the excitement of receiving the box of traps by parcel post.

It seemed to take an eternity for the nights to turn cool. Monty said we needed four nights with below-freezing temperatures for the skunk pelts to become prime. There was a sea-

son on muskrats that started November 1. By mid-October Monty allowed it was time to begin taking skunks.

In the weeks that followed, the old man spent many hours teaching me the lore of the fur trapper. He taught me to identify tracks and how to find the paths of small animals. I spent hours learning pelt preparation. I believed him to be the best trapper and one of the finest men God ever created.

We sold our furs to a local fur buyer two weeks before Christmas. I had two skunks and four-teen muskrats. Monty beamed when the fur buyer gave me three ten-dollar bills for my catch. His take was much larger.

Seven years later I was a Private First Class in the United States Marine Corps in Camp Pendleton, California. In late October there was a P.S. to my mother's letter that brought tears to my eyes. She wrote, "Oh, yes, Bert Montgomery died last week." That was all. It was enough.

To Have a Friend

To advance on our life's journey requires that we interact with other people. All of us have experienced people who have been our adversaries, and fortunately we have also experienced those who have been our supporters, as Monty was to me.

At the core of our being all humans are the same. We are, in fact, brothers and sisters. Because we are prone to judge the visible, the external, the materialistic, we have great difficulty with the statement, "All people are created equal." It is amazing what we see when we seek to see only the good, only the Christ, in others. It is also amazing what others have the opportunity to see in us when we do.

Perhaps one of the most enjoyable of human events happens when an adversary becomes a supporter, a brother, a friend. When this happens *A Course In Miracles* tells us, "All heaven rejoices." Let us examine a process that will allow us to experience more and stronger supportive relationships and heal some of those we have damaged by fear-based words and deeds.

Regardless of the reason two people are in communication or the reason a group was formed (two or more are a group), trust-based relationships are absolutely essential to have a happy, healthy, productive human group, whether it's a family group, work group, sports team, or other. If we are willing to peel off and cast aside the layers of fear-based prejudice, we will find at the core of our being a desire to have loving relationships with as many people as time in our lives will allow us to accommodate. It is important, beyond the ability of most of us to comprehend, to rid ourselves of fear. When we do, differences in race, ethnicity, beliefs, or sexuality will not be an impediment to our relationships.

Because of our fear of being hurt in some way by someone, many one-to-one relationships are built slowly or are blocked entirely and never evolve. This is especially true if one or both persons have been deeply hurt in a previous relationship and have not experienced the healing release of forgiveness.

By our words or actions we may communicate to people that they must earn our trust. Because of our fear many potentially beautiful relationships never get beyond the level of acquaintance. I suggest we consider accepting the teaching, based on scientific study, which states:

> *"It is better to trust a person and not let fear block the possibility of a supportive relationship, unless one has clear reason not to trust."*

Marital Love

Making Love—A Misnomer

As difficult as it may be, it seems important for us to attempt to differentiate between love-based relationships and relationships based on sexual attraction. The difficulty has been created because we have labeled emotionally driven sexuality as love. It is very difficult for people in our culture to accept that mature, lasting love between a man and a woman is a decision and not a hormonally driven attraction, which is more accurately defined as lust.

It is not wrong nor bad to be "in lust" with another person, it is simply a sexually driven motivation. We get into difficulty by expecting this sexual attraction to last a lifetime. *It will not!* But if we are willing to expend energy on a relationship, which began with the short-term beauty and passion of sexual attraction, it is entirely possible to *build* a long-term, solidly beautiful relationship that **can** last a lifetime.

Let us further consider marital love, which almost invariably begins with "falling in lust." Being in lust is a marvelous, ecstatic, quite insane, and totally desirable state. However, there is one problem: Our egos at such times are totally defenseless and in danger of being squashed by a look, a word, or a snub from the person of our intentions. Few among us have not suffered this pain.

Typically our first love, often called puppy love is a very real and painful part of growing up. First loves are almost always entered into with reckless abandon when hormones are running wild. Only rarely are they more than a short-term learning experience, for many of us a most painful one. We romantics think of this as pain of the heart—certainly it runs deep. But more careful examination clearly shows us it is a wound to the ego, reflected in fear-based, emotional pain.

When two immature egos find each other and conclude, "This is the best I can do to fulfill my incompleteness," sexually, socially, financially, and so on, they fall in lust and think it is love because of mislabeling by our society. Sometimes it can last for several years. But be very sure, **if you fall in lust, you will fall out of lust!** It is at this point that uninformed, immature people give up the relationship and begin to search again for another half to make them a whole.

If we can accept that we are not our bodies and we are complete unto ourselves, we can truly make a decision to love our mate. Mature love is not devoid of conjugal satisfaction, quite the contrary. When sex is shared between two people who have decided to love each other, it is love-based giving, not needs-based taking. Mature, loving people can validate the following simple, spiritual truth with each sexual act:

"Giving and receiving are the same."

Parental Love

It may be even more difficult to accept that loving our children is also a decision. **This decision goes far beyond the instinctive nurturing and protection of our offspring. This behavior is provided**

by nature to all members of the animal kingdom for survival of the species.

Certainly it is not wrong to nurture and protect our children. No one would argue that point. It is the same thing the mother grizzly bear does. However to love our children is a decision. **It is obvious from information in the news media that not all parents make that decision.**

It is not always easy to love our children. Loving them requires us to make some of the most difficult decisions civilized people are called upon to make. For example, when a child is transitioning into adulthood, **to remove nurturing and protection, when it will contribute to the growth and autonomy the child is most surely love!**

Healthy, heterosexual girls typically develop feelings of competition with and alienation from their mothers in the early teen years. Boys have this same difficulty with their fathers, typically in their mid- to late teens. The parent who is controlled by fear, rather than love, cannot graciously allow the child to become his or her own person. **The agony created by this misunderstanding of what parental love is, is pandemic in our society.**

From Separation to Relationship

We will now consider building relationships on a much broader scale. Relationships that have a high trust component contribute greatly to the progress of mankind. The peace of the world and the mutually beneficial commerce of the world depends heavily upon such relationships. To be happy, successful, prosperous, and healthy are certainly worthwhile personal goals. However, the fulfillment of these goals, just as with world commerce, depends heavily on our ability to build

long-lasting, trust-based relationships in our professional lives, our personal lives, and our spiritual lives.

Let us begin exploring a modality for understanding this dynamic process, which can help us move
more quickly and surely from separation to relationship. *(Please carefully review Diagram 1.)*

Separation in our day-to-day world needs little clarification. Probably all of us have felt alone or even lone-
ly in a crowd. However, if we are into spiritual, love-
based inclusion, we may never feel separation or loneli-
ness, with or without the physical presence of others.

Acquaintance

We probably shrug off the need for any elaboration
on becoming acquainted with another person as relatively unimportant. Typically a mutual acquaintance
introduces us or we introduce ourselves. But there is
much more for us to consider each time we meet
someone new. If we are aware, if we truly want it, and
if we seek it, each new acquaintance has the potential
of becoming a beautiful addition to our lives.

A Course in Miracles tells us, "Every encounter is
a holy encounter." That can be said another way:
"We do not meet another person by accident." We
cannot know at the outset if this encounter will last a
few seconds or a lifetime. If we keep that in mind, we
may be more inclined to be attentive during these
important events in our lives.

Many of us set ourselves up to reduce the possibility of a comfortable and pleasant first meeting by
failing to remember the name of the person to whom
we were just introduced. We may often say, "I just
can't remember names." We will not go into the psychology of self-fulfilling prophecy, but I encourage
you to consider the message or instruction you are

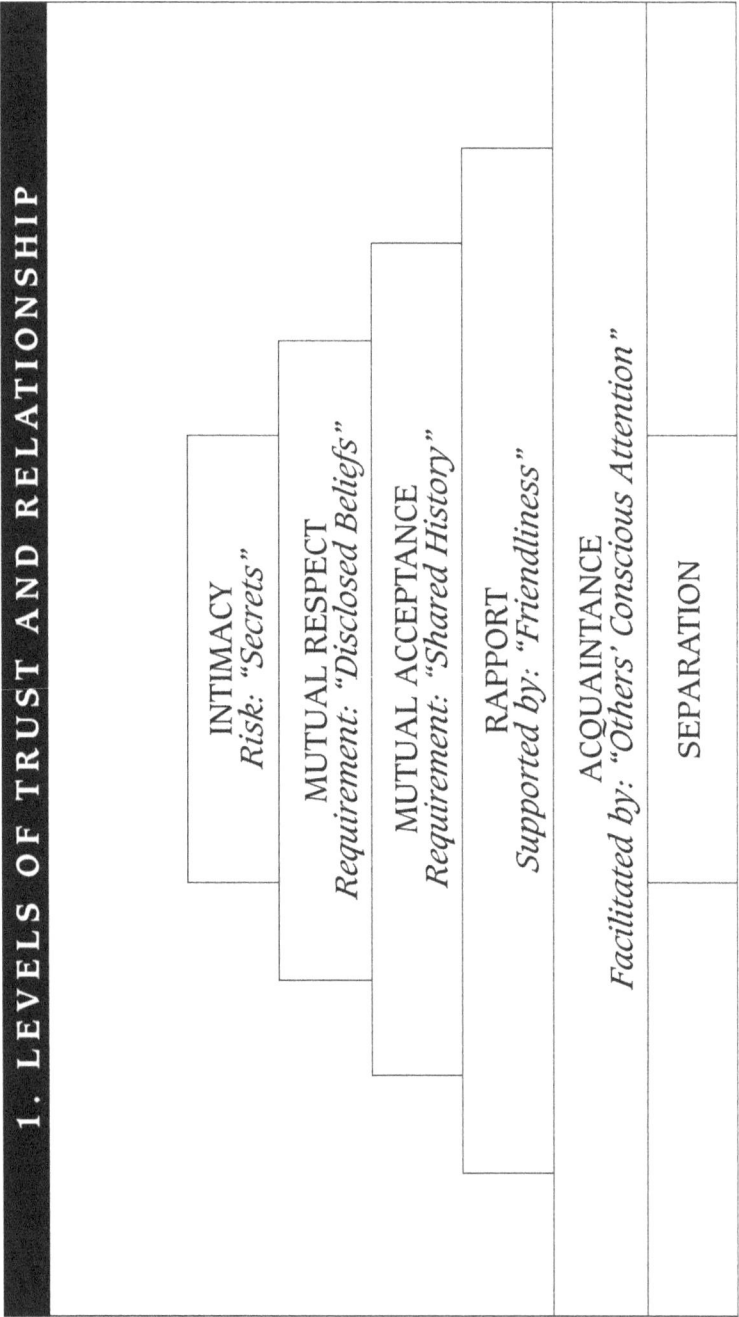

1. LEVELS OF TRUST AND RELATIONSHIP

INTIMACY
Risk: "Secrets"

MUTUAL RESPECT
Requirement: "Disclosed Beliefs"

MUTUAL ACCEPTANCE
Requirement: "Shared History"

RAPPORT
Supported by: "Friendliness"

ACQUAINTANCE
Facilitated by: "Others' Conscious Attention"

SEPARATION

sending your subconscious mind every time you say you can't remember names. If you want to remember people's names, the recommendation is to stop saying that! Additionally, if we train ourselves to use the love-based behavior of being others-conscious, rather than the fear-based behavior of being self-conscious during the introduction, we will find it much easier to remember the person's name.

Let us be clear that the objective of building a relationship can be summarized quite simply as building trust. **If you have one you have the other.** I fully realize there are some big names in behavioral science who disagree, but in my opinion it is not complicated. It can be considered as a five-step process—the sequential steps are:

- ✧ **Acquaintance**
- ✧ **Rapport**
- ✧ **Mutual acceptance**
- ✧ **Mutual respect**
- ✧ **Intimacy**

The lubrication that allows us to move smoothly from one level of trust/relationship to the other is information—very specific information, **about each other.** This information is best described as **self-disclosure.** Now please understand the following: **The longer lasting, more intimate we want the relationship to become, the riskier is the level of self-disclosure.** More about this in a bit—first I shall clarify my use of the words, *intimate* and *intimacy.*

Under the right conditions sexual or physical intimacy is a wonderful thing to work on, **but that is not what we are talking about.** The intimacy we are talking about is accurately described as, **emotional,**

mental, or spiritual. Yes, we are talking about love, not sex or romance. It is quite clear sexual activity does not require this intimacy, yet it is also evident this intimacy can enrich our sexual relationships.

Now let us focus on the risk factors associated with each level of growing toward intimacy. *(Please refer to the Levels of Trust and Relationship chart.)*

The first level on the pyramid, Acquaintance level, signifies the end of feelings of separation from the other individual. Though it is a common occurrence, there is much for us to consider each time we meet someone new. As suggested earlier, our very quality of life depends on relationships. Professional success most certainly depends on our ability to convert as many acquaintances as possible to stronger/higher levels of relationship.

Love Affairs Measured in Microtime

There are almost unlimited opportunities for us to meaningfully touch the lives of others and be touched by them in very brief encounters. These microevents in our lives may be encounters that began with an introduction or with a brief eye contact and a smile. For example:

> *Two participants of a personal growth group arrived a few hours before our departure time to the retreat location. I was delighted to have them assist me with the job of buying groceries for eight people for the three-day retreat. As we approached the check out counter with three heavily loaded carts, I noticed the clerk's facial expression. It was as if this was the last straw. Our eyes met briefly, and she knew I was aware of her despair. She made a half-hearted attempt at a welcoming comment.*

We again had eye contact, and I asked, "How long have you been standing there checking out groceries?" She told me her shift was nearly over.

I said, "I'll bet your feet hurt and you are tired."

She quickly replied, "Right on both counts!"

The warm, lighthearted conversation that followed was enjoyed by everyone in the immediate area.

Two other examples of the microlove affair:

The final preparation activity for the week-long pack trip was an early morning stop at the ice cream store, the only place dry ice was available. A few dollars' worth of this precious commodity would keep our steaks from thawing out until the final night on the trail.

Two elderly ladies were attending the store. There was a pleasant exchange of comments when I answered their question regarding my need for the dry ice. After specifying the required number of pounds, I removed a five-dollar bill and three one dollar bills from my money clip. I laid the money on top of the cash register as the ladies finished wrapping the ice in several layers of newspaper. One of them rang up the total: seven dollars and eighty cents. She picked up the money, stammered and looked perplexed. She said, "Sir, the amount was $7.80."

I said, "Yes, that's fine." I expected her to give me my change.

Instead she said,"Sir, you didn't give me enough money." I responded by saying I was sure I had given her eight dollars. In the awkwardness that followed she showed me the three one dollar bills. She appeared genuinely stressed.

I said, "Not to worry, here is another five dollars, and I'll leave my business card. If you come up five dollars long today you can just mail it to me."

She appeared greatly relieved and said, "Thank you for trusting me."

I was leaving the store when she gleefully shouted, "Oh, here it is." The bill had fallen to the floor. The appreciative and kindly look in the old woman's eyes as she returned my money was worth multiples of the five dollars.

Near the end of the trip six days later, eleven very hungry, unshaven men entered a small cafe in a tiny mountain village in central Colorado, just before closing time. The only people in the cafe were the owner, who did the cooking, and a small, shy fifteen-year-old girl who was the waitress. She seemed nervous and unsure of her ability to handle such a large, boisterous group. We were just returning from a most enjoyable pack trip in the Flattops Wilderness Area.

With eye contact, smiles, and effort she became more comfortable. There was a large, hand-made sign on the wall touting the homemade apple pie with special emphasis on the size of the servings. After the main course every man at the table ordered pie. When she returned, empty handed, she was again uncomfortable. She said to me, "I'm sorry. There is only one pie left. Now what do we do?"

I said, "Tell the cook to cut it into twelve pieces, one for each of us and one for you. We'll all have plenty!" We all laughed and everyone at the table agreed that was a good solution.

After leaving the money for the check and a tip on the table, I was about to leave when she spontaneously gave me a hug and a kiss on the cheek. She said, "Thank you so much for help-ing me get through my first day as a waitress."

We can all enjoy many tremendously joyful, very short "love affairs" with a stranger. These efforts can bring joy to both people in what might otherwise have been a drab and colorless day. The only require-ment is a willingness to smile, make eye contact, and risk letting people know you are a loving person. **And it helps to remember their names.**

Rapport

All of us have had the enjoyable experience of walking away from an introduction, which achieved the acquaintance level with someone, genuinely look-ing forward to our next encounter with that person.

We can think of it in terms of good vibes, good chemistry, or **rapport.**

However, there is no assurance rapport will develop after acquaintance has occurred. Some people seem to be able to create rapport with almost everyone they meet. This makes them well qualified to be greeters, hosts or hostesses, receptionists, and so on. It is very important for us to understand there is no magic in this ability. These are **learned** skills!

We can accurately speculate on some of the behavioral and personality traits of the good greeters. They probably have a strong need for the approval of others—they want to please people. They genuinely like people, and they will readily say they want others to like them. If these needs are coupled with strong feelings of self-worth, the approval need will be an accelerator to progressing up the relationship pyramid.

Taking a Risk to Gain Acceptance

If we want to see a relationship grow, it is helpful to know there is another minor risk factor for us to work through if we are to advance from the level of **rapport** to the level of **mutual acceptance.** The entire relationship model can be looked upon as a stair-stepped continuum of increasing levels of trust, facilitated by deepening levels of self-disclosure. Each level of disclosure is a level of risk. The risk that facilitates mutual acceptance is letting the other person know who you are by exchanging such information as family background, education, career experiences, and so on.

If I had the opportunity to build a relationship with you, dear reader, as I disclosed information about my life (as in this book), I would also seek to know who you are. As you discover who I am, you will find that I was a poor student in high school and never attended college or participated in formal studies related to things of which I write. You will also discover I am a divorced and remarried man. The risk is, as you know more about my history, you may choose to discount me and my work because of my past, including my lack of higher education. But if I want the relationship to progress, these are risks I must take.

Another of the simple spiritual truths, which supports the first sentence in the introduction of this book is:

"Truth sets you free."

Truth often requires courage and may at times be painful, but it never encumbers us or entraps us.

We usually present our histories in normal interactions over a long period of time. If our histories do not raise the barrier of fear, our relationship will grow in an unencumbered manner. But until I know something about who you are and vice versa, mutual acceptance is not likely to happen.

Advancing to the Level of Mutual Respect

There is no guarantee that telling each other who we are will lead to mutual respect. When we get to know one another, we will invariably discover differences and similarities in our values. Our similarities in values will serve as an attracting force. We may continue to grow together in spite of the differences, or because of them we may grow apart. It is a matter of choice.

Developing mutual respect not only requires that we become familiar with each other's histories, but also with personal beliefs and values. To respect you, is in fact, to respect your beliefs and values. **Yet, it is**

**not necessary for us to have the same beliefs
and values to respect each other.** For example, I
share a deep and long lasting love and respect with a
friend who is a deacon in a Southern Baptist Church.
He will not drink an alcoholic beverage under any circumstance. I do not share that value. However, we
also know each of us has a deep and abiding faith in
God. Another of my dear friends is a Jewish psychia-
trist. We consider ourselves as brothers and have a
loving relationship. Our love and respect for each other
exists in spite of our differences of belief about Jesus.

The Factor of Equality

Research psychologists have been studying mutual
respect for many years. A highly regarded researcher,
George C. Homans, came to the following conclusion:

*"When people meet in face-to-face interaction they
will come to respect one another, if they meet in a
state of equality."*

Many dentists and physicians have found when
they treat their staffs and patients as equals, communication is dramatically improved. This is accomplished
by giving up the title "Doctor" and by suggesting to
their staff and patients that they address each other on
a first-name basis. That difference in communication
greatly reduces the status hierarchical difference
imposed by formality.

Risking to Strengthen Trust and
Grow into Intimacy

As suggested earlier, we are using the word intimacy here in the psychological and spiritual sense. There
is little doubt that psychological and spiritual intimacy

can enhance sexual intimacy, yet it is also true that sexual activity does not require intimacy. It is sad but true—some marriages do not achieve intimacy.

People who are willing to take responsibility for themselves will grow in the ability to be intimate because they are intimate with themselves. Self-intimacy means no more than being honest with yourself. One of the difficulties of achieving intimacy with another person is that it requires both people in the relationship to be intimate at the same time. It is indeed a choice, which suggests that we must be selective with whom we will take this risk. When we share our secrets with true intimates, we trust they will not use the information against us. They will say such things as, "I understand—you couldn't help it," or "You just made a mistake."

Those willing to take the risk by taking off their masks and being authentic will open the door to the strongest of relationships and will come to find their secrets do not shock a loving person. It is the path that leads to knowing ourselves and others at the most fulfilling level.

Growth toward relationship is not necessarily a step-by-step, sequential occurrence. However, to have an enduring intimate relationship, a high level of trust is essential. Trust starts to grow very early in the relationship-building process, and we know it requires a measure of interpersonal comfort, which requires some measure of shared values. However, to attain a higher level of trust requires a higher level of risk taking.

Please keep in mind the earlier admonition to employ the simple spiritual truth: **"Truth sets you free."** Now examine the secrets you have that you do not tell others about. In your most honest assessment, what do you suppose would happen if your best friends knew your secret? Do you think they would still love you? Is it possible they know it anyway?

Please understand I am not suggesting you should or shouldn't have personal secrets. But it does seem important for you to consider the costs or penalties of maintaining them. Secrets are our hidden self. If a person has a great number of them, he or she must spend considerable amounts of energy protecting that large area of hidden self. To protect those secrets, he or she will seek to avoid some subjects or become evasive if they arise in conversation. This can raise suspicion for the other person in the relationship.

It is possible to have what we might consider an intimate relationship and still maintain some secrets. However, if we have a great number of secrets or more serious secrets, we are deluding ourselves if we believe the relationship has true intimacy where trust flourishes.

Let us consider trust for a bit. One avenue of gaining an understanding of what trust is, is to review what it is not. For this purpose we can select "suspicion," which is one of trust's direct opposites. From a simple comparison of trust and suspicion we can develop a useful formula for enhancing or restoring trust:

*To increase or restore trust in any relationship, identify everything **you do** that might contribute to suspicion, and stop doing it.*

Suspicion and trust are co-variables. They are such strong opposites, one must decrease for the other to increase. **When seeking to restore trust in a relationship, it is useful to remember suspicion is fear based and trust is love based. It can be very helpful to tell the other person of your** desire to increase trust and how you propose to work on it!

Relationship Insurance to Maintain and Enhance Trust

The concept I am going to introduce to you next is another very simple process. To provide us an example and facilitate clarification of the process, let us assume you have a marriage relationship you wish to maintain and strengthen. If you choose to purchase relationship insurance, or in this case, marriage insurance, here is your assignment:

At an appropriate time, when you and your spouse are alone, ask him or her one, or all of the following questions: (Note: Be ready for a shocked reaction.)

- *"How am I doing as your wife (or husband)?"*

- *"What could I do that would make our marriage better for you?"*

- *"What suggestions do you have for me—what would you like me to do differently?"*

The following statement is the cardinal rule to consider before asking any of the above questions: **"Don't ask if you don't want to know!"**

What you are really asking your spouse to do is to function as your *marriage consultant!* If your spouse accepts, great and if he or she chooses to reciprocate, so much the better! But it is very important to the process for you to understand there is no requirement for your spouse to do so. If you and your spouse thoughtfully and openly respond to the questions, you will be achieving a more intimate relationship.

Consultancy Relationships Expanded

I strongly endorse the usefulness of the consultancy process in manager/employee relationships at all levels in business and industry. It matters little, if at all, who initiates the dialogue. Yet, just imagine how much easier it is for the manager to provide constructive, corrective information to an employee who has opened the communications door by asking for performance feedback.

Family Communications

Shortly after I delivered a lecture in Madison, Wisconsin, I was visiting with a friend who had heard me speak on a number of occasions. Immediately after we greeted each other he said, "Bud, you didn't tell the Michael story."

I said, "No, I didn't. I thought maybe people were tired of hearing it."

His strong feelings were unmistakable as he said, "You must include that story—it is much too important to leave out. That story has made a significant difference in my life because it helped me so much in my relationship with my two sons!"

The following conversations between my son and me (the "Michael story") had been included in my lecture presentations for several years. Over a period of time I told the story less and less frequently and finally dropped it from my repertoire. I have now reincluded it in my presentations.

The Michael Story

One Saturday several years ago my son Michael and I were busy transporting two stock trailer loads of horses to a leased pasture about twenty miles from our home. Michael was ten years old at the time. As anyone familiar with horses knows loading the animals can sometimes try one's patience if the horses haven't been in a trailer for some months.

Following the difficulty of loading uncooperative horses, there were just Michael and me in the truck as we drove to the pasture with the first load. During the drive I said, "Son, I would like to make a deal with you."

He asked what I had in mind, and I said, "I would like you and me to become each other's consultant. What do you think about that?"

His immediate response was, "You'll have to tell me what you mean."

I explained if he agreed to be my consultant, I could ask him how I was doing as his dad and he would give me his opinion, and I said, "If you want me to be your consultant, you can ask me how you are doing as my son, and I'll tell you my opinion. What do you think of the idea?"

He gave me a very mature answer for a ten-year-old. He said, "I'll have to think about it."

About three hours later, after unloading the

second group of horses, we were finally headed home. It was quiet in the truck when Michael said, "I'm ready to tell you now, Dad."
I said, "Tell me what?"

"I thought you wanted me to be your consultant."

I said, "Oh, yes, how am I doing as your Dad?"

The suppressed tone of his voice communicated deep feelings as he said, "I think you oughta let down a little."

He did not have to elaborate—I had leaned on him pretty hard several times that day.

"Son, I appreciate you telling me that. I know what you are saying, and I promise to work on it."

Then I said with great expectation, "Now, do you want me to be your consultant?"

His one word answer was quick and very clear, "Nope!" That was the end of the conversation.

However, about two weeks later Michael and I were going somewhere else in the truck when he said, "Dad, when I get in junior high do you think any kid will try to sell me dope?"

I said, "Well, Mike, I'm not sure. When I was in junior high, we didn't have any dope. But from all I hear, I suppose some kid will try to sell you some."

He said, "That's what I thought."

I asked, "If some kid tries to sell you dope, what are you going to tell him?"

Mike responded immediately and said, "I've thought about it, and I've decided to tell him I've got my own dealer!"

I was tempted to chuckle at his ten-year-old decision making. But the gravity of the discussion ruled out any levity. Instead it became awfully quiet in the truck. It was quiet for at least three miles until I finally said, "If some kid tries to sell you dope and you tell him you've got your own dealer, what are you going to say if he tells you he'll cut your dealer's price?"

Michael thought for a few seconds and then with audible tension in his voice said, "I never thought of that!"

"How would it be if you just told him you aren't into dope?" I asked.

He responded with another question, "That won't make him mad, will it?"

I said, "I don't think so, and maybe he won't bug you any more."

After thinking about my words for several

*moments he said, almost to himself, "That's a
better answer." And that was the end of that
conversation.*

Although I cannot say with certainty, I sincerely
believe the conversation we had two weeks earlier
when we were hauling horses planted the seeds for
him to ask me to be his consultant. Since that time
Michael and I have had many conversations about
this subject.

For example, when Michael was fourteen, we
went on a "Lads and Dads" backpack trip. During
the outing we had a few hours for just the two of us,
high on a mountainside in Colorado. We had planned
our consulting time a day earlier, so we had time for
preparation. When we arrived at the place he had
preselected he said, "I don't need consulting this time
Dad. I just want to talk about some stuff."

I asked him what he had in mind, and he said,
"I want to talk about Mormons, suicide, beer, Jesus,
and sex."

He wanted to talk about Mormons because a
Mormon family had moved into our area some
months before and we had become good friends.
He wanted to talk about suicide because the sixteen-
year-old brother of one of his close friends had
recently committed suicide. I talked of the possible
selfishness of suicide because of the pain it creates for
others. Michael had lots of questions, some of which
I could not answer. It was easy to tell him so when
that happened. I gave him mostly an historical perspective of Jesus. He knows today my response
would be much more personal and intimate. We
talked about the difficulties alcohol has presented to
our society and how difficult it is to control on a per-

sonal basis. His questions regarding sex were easily answered. It was a priceless, beautiful afternoon.

I feel sure if anyone were to ask him today who his consultant is he would answer, "My Dad."

The concept of two people becoming involved in a consulting relationship is not magic. It is simply two people who are consciously and with forethought committed to becoming more intimate. The requirement is to help each other by utilizing love-based, open communications. It may well be the best activity possible to maintain and enhance any relationship, while at the same time appropriately using the relationship as a valuable personal resource.

FINDING BY ASKING

I know a man who knows all the words
and all the right things to say.
His clothes are just right and he smiles,
but still he's not happy today.

Something is missing, and he knows not what
for he tries to do the right thing.
But his need to impress and his perfect dress
make it hard to feel life's sting.

He knows hurt, but not where to turn,
though he's been told many times.
He seeks solace from man-made things
and doesn't hear the chimes

That ring out each day and surround us at play
or work as the case may be.
The door is ajar, but each one must knock
for only we have the key.

To save us from sadness and life forlorn
and turmoil and difficult pain,
Our Helpers are waiting to supply our lack
and put it right again.

Just ask, then listen, and soon you will say
God keeps every promise. We must only pray.
The words aren't important, but deep from our heart,
We're not alone and must do our part.

Chapter Four

To Clarify
Our Mission

Meekness has awesome power.
It allows us to accept guidance.

❖ ❖ ❖

Our Creator has a great plan for each of us,
which can only be thwarted by our free will
to choose against it.

❖ ❖ ❖

When the student is ready the teacher will appear.
*When the **teacher** is ready the students will appear.*

❖ ❖ ❖

To teach love overtly by words or quietly by example
may well be man's highest calling.

All Are Called...
"If you believe in God and if your work
becomes part of your worship, you will
never work again."
—Charles M. Sorenson, D.D., Ph.D.

I WAS SEVENTEEN *and about to graduate from high school. Early in the winter my father had undergone back surgery and wouldn't begin working again until June. I suggested to my mother that I drop out of school and work full-time to help the family. She wouldn't hear of it so I experienced the bitter taste of the welfare program, Aid to Dependent Children. Immature pride lead me to detest the free cheese, powdered eggs, and other commodities.*

I rather doubted that any of the boys I knew owned two suits. I had decided to quietly ask around because I didn't have one to wear to the graduation ceremony. At about the time I was starting to become concerned, I received a note in school one afternoon. The note directed me to visit the local tailor shop after class.

The tailor fitted me with a beautiful new suit. He told me it had all been paid for and that he had promised not to tell me who my benefactor was. I have never known whom to thank. However, I do thank God for that compassionate and generous person.

❖ ❖ ❖

The teenage boy stopped his bicycle, dismounted, and laid it on its side. He ran to help the four-year-old who had fallen from his tricycle.

❖ ❖ ❖

During a routine visit to the dental office Edna discovered she needed to have a tooth crowned. The usual price for a crown was $550. As a retired schoolteacher, she had no dental insurance and very little money. Without mentioning the usual fee the *dentist, quoted her a price of $300 and sincerely apologized that it was so expensive.*

✧ ✧ ✧

Ed was nearing 80 years old. He was physically active in spite of a battle with cancer for three years. When he didn't attend the meeting of the Rod and Gun Club, the secretary was asked to call him to make sure he was OK. He was surprised that someone cared.

In each of the preceding vignettes someone was functioning as one of God's teachers, probably without being aware of it. To accept the mission or work of being one of God's teachers does not require any special preparation or the approval of any other person. If you choose to consider accepting this assignment, I suggest it will be helpful if you can also accept two very simple, irrefutable laws.

✧ *You can't not be a student.*
✧ *You can't not be a teacher.*

You will either be a good teacher and student, a mediocre one or a poor one. How well you fulfill the laws is a matter of your choice. Your age, education, life circumstances, level of motivation, or your spirituality or lack thereof do not matter. You are a teacher, and you are student. Consider the young mother with her firstborn. Is it possible the baby will not be the mother's teacher?

If you elect to become one of God's teachers, it does not matter if you live in a mansion on a hill, a house with a picket fence, a ghetto, a shanty, or have no home at all. It matters not if you are a student, a housewife, unemployed, a craftsman, a prisoner, a laborer, or a professional.

To become God's active teacher, however, it is necessary that you be willing to teach forgiveness and acceptance rather than judgment, condemnation, and separation.

An Event of Certainty

After a failed marriage, my youngest daughter came home and entered college. She and her one-year-old son returned to live with my wife and me and our ten-year-old son. They lived with us for about five years, until she graduated. I was over 50 years old when they moved in with us. Who do you suppose was one of my most influential teachers during those years? Yes, indeed, my teacher was that small bundle of energy, emotions, confusion, and needs—my grandson, Ryan.

I am absolutely certain I was also his teacher. Ryan freely volunteered to spend countless hours with me in my large vegetable garden, to tend horses, to repair fences, and to do the myriad other tasks on a small ranch. Do you see that there was no way I could have avoided being his teacher or he could have avoided being mine?

God's Teacher: Your Choice

Yes, indeed, you cannot avoid being a teacher throughout your lifetime. However, being one of God's teachers is significantly different. It is a matter of personal choice. I believe and support the spiritual teaching from *A Course in Miracles*:

> *"All are called to be God's teachers, but few choose to respond or accept the responsibility."*

It is very important for us to keep in mind that it is not a matter of all or nothing. I suggest any time you perform a loving act you are functioning as one of God's teachers. However, to become a master teacher requires much more of all of the elements than being a novice. It requires such elements as energy, study, commitment, time, and willingness to risk disapproval or even rejection by one's peers and perhaps one's own family.

It is true that before one can become a master, one must first be a novice. If one accepts the challenge of being a novice teacher, one is decidedly on a spiritual path. It has long been known, if you really want to learn something, teach it! When the teacher ceases to learn, as much or more than her or his students, it may well be time for the teacher to move further along the path. *We teach best that which we are in the process of learning!*

Conditions That Can Help

Please consider the following statement:

Everyone is in the right place in his or her life situation.

This is true regardless of whether he or she is happy or sad, rich or poor, healthy or sick, black, white, yellow, or brown, a homosexual or a heterosexual. It matters not at all if one lives in the city or the country, in the wilderness or civilization. It doesn't matter at all if one is Christian, Jew, Muslim, Hindu, Buddhist, agnostic, or atheist. **No one is wrong or in the wrong place, just different, or in a different place.** Even if you are dissatisfied with where you are, you are not in the wrong place. It is the right place, the only place, from which you can begin to change.

102 • THE RIGHT PLACE

A requirement to be one of God's teachers is a little willingness to strive to overcome one of mankind's most common behaviors: judgment. We must struggle not only against judgment of another person, as good or bad, right or wrong, better or worse, **but also against judgment of any situation!**

The Fallacy of Judging Situations:
Where you are AT is the right place.

As a management communications consultant I am a member of a team of five people. About five years ago during a staff meeting one of the group said to me, "Bud, what do you want to do? We don't care what you want to do, but we want to help you do it, so we need to know."

Another member of the group said, "We know a number of your friends are planning retirement in the next few years and we want to know what your plans are."

I responded very quickly, "I have no idea!" After more discussion I agreed to think about it and give them an answer as soon as I had one.

A couple of weeks later at a planning session, I was asked the same question again. Again I told them I didn't have a clue. They then suggested I take a few days off, go fishing, and think about it. I immediately accepted that assignment. No coaxing was required!

A few days later I loaded my backpack. With my dog Bham, I headed for one of my favorite timberline lakes in Colorado's White River National Forest for three days of fly fishing and contemplation. The fishing was great. Each day, after blessing its spirit, I killed one fish for Bham and me to eat and I gently released all of the other beautiful native cutthroat trout I caught.

(*NOTE:* Regarding blessing the spirit of the fish before killing it to eat, I live by this teaching: *"Bless the spirit of this fish (or any other animal) that is giving up its life to contribute to my life."* The practice is congruent with the teachings of Oriental, Jewish, and Native American cultures.)

Indeed the fishing was great, but the contemplation was unproductive. So I returned home renewed and refreshed but with nothing to report.

However, I did continue to think about the question. About two months later I again had an opportunity to devote time to thinking about what I wanted to do with the remainder of my life. That, I think, was the real question.

Life Relived

This opportunity came in an elk hunting camp. I am unashamedly a hunter, though I no longer have a strong need to kill another elk. So, during each of the five days of the hunt, after tidying up the camp, I took my rifle and walked about a mile to a magnificent outcropping of rock. It was on a sunny south slope and had a natural rock chair with a backrest. From this vantage point I could see the vast panorama of a mountain valley and a natural elk crossing, which went unused during the hours I sat in this lookout. Thus, each day, I had several hours to think about "The Question."

I had thought about it so much with no progress that I was at a loss as to how to proceed. Then it occurred to me that perhaps I would receive direction if I mentally relived my life, as completely as I could, from my earliest memories. I cannot say how many hours this activity consumed, but it was a considerable number. I took many mental side trips, some of them joyful, some of them painful, some evoking feelings of old sadness, some bringing back the memories of old fears. Many times I fought back tears. Please bear with me as I tell you about a few of the side trips.

Memories of Earlier Years

I clearly remembered my fourth birthday and the guilt I felt because I did not appreciate my gift. My parents gave me a kiddie car. I wanted one with pedals—a tricycle. I remembered my first day in school. My mother didn't accompany me, my older sister Wanda was my guide. After taking a seat in Miss Rickey's first grade class,

I looked around and realized I knew only one other
person in the room, a boy from our Sunday school.
There were about twenty-five children in the class. I
graduated from high school with almost half of them.
Many of them were involved in a large number of the
memories I relived.

As I sat on that rock I remembered many of the
planned episodes of my life as well as many that
were unplanned, at least not consciously by me.
One such unplanned episode follows.

Evolvement of a Loner

During my high school years I enjoyed the reputation of being a competent hunter, fisherman, and trapper
of fur-bearing animals. These were largely solo activities.
I spent most of my winter weekends moving my traps to
a new and hopefully more productive location. I shall
never forget the excitement of visiting my muskrat traps
the next morning at daylight after such a move.

I made two attempts to break out of the self-
imposed isolation from my peers in high school. I
tried out for the junior class play and went out for
football that same year. I really felt rejected when the
teacher who selected the cast for the play, selected
another boy for the role I wanted. I crawled back into
my shell and again withdrew from any but the most
necessary interaction with other students.

My involvement in the football program was even
more esteem reducing. In the two years I played, our
team won only one game each year, and those wins
were against small parochial schools that were not in
our league. One of our wins was by six points, the
other by one point. A typical score in a league game
was 56 to 6. Our worst drubbing was 72 to 0. Both
years when the final gun went off signaling the last

game was over, as I walked off the playing field I was so relieved I cried. It was an emotionally devastating time. I didn't watch a complete National Football League game on television until I was 40 years old.

These factors, in combination with a poor academic record, contributed to feelings of self-worthlessness. This low self-esteem might have contributed to the feelings of lack of purpose that I experienced when I finished high school. My feeling of having no purpose and no place where I really belonged ended abruptly, three months after it began. The following story is the unplanned episode of how that happened.

The Hidden Agenda and an Unplanned Turning Point

One Friday afternoon my friend Jimmy showed up unexpectedly at the construction project where I was working. I was surprised to see him and accepted without question his explanation that he just wanted to spend the weekend with me and would bring me back to the job site on Sunday evening.

On the long ride home we talked of many things. Did I like my job? Did I miss home cooking? How long was this job going to last? However, it wasn't long until he disclosed his real agenda for providing me this unexpected gift of transportation.

"Bud," he said, "I just got my notice from the draft board, and unless I can qualify for a deferment I'll be in the Army in less than two months. My chances for a deferment are slim and none." (The date was early August 1950, and the Korean War was just heating up.)

Without waiting for a reply from me he said, "Let's join the Navy. We've said we wanted to do that since we were kids. We could go in on their buddy system and have a bunch of fun. What do you say?"

I was really taken off guard by Jimmy's proposal. I hadn't even thought of joining the military. The construction project on which I was working was in the heart of a prime waterfowl hunting area, and I was eagerly looking forward to the fall hunting. It would have been awkward to shut off the conversation by telling Jimmy what I was thinking. However, I had an ace in the hole—a way out, which wouldn't hurt my friend.

"Well, Jim," I said, "you know I won't be eighteen for more than a month, so I would have to have my parents' permission."

Jimmy responed quickly, "Let's go ask your Dad."

My father had said on a number of occasions that he would never, under any circumstances, sign a paper giving his permission for me to join any military service. So I was quite comfortable saying, "Sure, let's do just that."

When we approached my dad with the idea, he said, "Well, if that's what you want to do I guess it's OK."

I couldn't believe my ears! My father's response shocked me to say the least. A short while later Jimmy and I were driving to Pueblo, Colorado, to the recruiting station.

After recording our names and addresses, the Navy recruiter said, "Boys, I have my quota for this period, so you will leave for the Naval Training Center in San Diego in about six weeks."

Jimmy's response was, "We want to go now!"

"Sorry," the recruiter said, "I can't take you now."

Jimmy turned to me and said, "Bud, let's join the Marines."

The Marine recruiting office was only one flight up. Wouldn't you know it, the Marine recruiter had openings!

Going with the Flow

It was almost as if I were being swept along by a fast-moving but invisible current. I had an almost fatalistic attitude about it all and went with the flow. My parents sponsored a good-bye party for us at the local Eagles Lodge, and in a few short days we were in Denver for the induction process.

Jimmy's last name started with a "B," which placed him near the front of a line of about fifty young men, as we began the day-long ordeal of physical, academic, and psychological testing. I was usually waiting in line when Jimmy emerged from a testing room. As he walked by on his way to the next test, he would say, "Bud, this is a piece of cake. Nothing to it."

Toward the end of the day, as I stood in the last line I saw Jimmy emerge from a room fully clothed. I was expecting his usual encouragement, but this time his comment was, "Bud, this last test was a tough one. I didn't make it—see ya around."

My last sight of Jimmy was watching him, from the rear, as he skipped down the steps of the Old Customs House in Denver on his way home. That was over forty years ago and I haven't seen him since. As a result I've never had the opportunity to tell him I wasn't angry, just surprised.

The next few weeks were a blur of activity as I

went through the physical and mental rigors of
Marine Boot Camp. I clearly remember thinking many
times, "It's just as well Jimmy didn't make it. I've got
all I can do to take care of myself."

Significantly for me, after joining the Marines I
immediately had a place where I belonged and was
very clear on my purpose. That sense of purpose and
being where I belong has never left me.

Back to the Rock Lookout

So I continued for those several days, sitting on the
rock outcropping and remembering and reliving the joys,
the sorrows, the excitement and the pain of my life. I
especially savored again experiencing each of my past
loves—from Betty Jo Brinlee in elementary school, to my
present wife, and all of the loves in between, even
though many, perhaps most of them, did not know of
my infatuation. Finally I advanced my life's events to
that exact moment in time, sitting on that rock.

What did I gain from this exercise, other than the
best possible mental television series I shall ever see?
As I sat on that rock, knowing I was in the right
place, I came to a major conclusion, which is an inte-
gral part of my life's credo:

*During my life I have been in some happy places
and some sad places, some difficult places and
some easy ones. Some were painful and some
were painless. Some were exciting, and some
were dull. Some places were very safe, and
some very dangerous. But never once, for one
second, have I ever been in the wrong place.*

The experience I gained while sitting on the rock
helped me clearly accept that I am incapable of judg-

ing a life situation or a turning point as good or bad. This is true, quite simply because I cannot know what happens next or the reason for the event.

I shall never forget reliving my memories. I heartily recommend it to everyone. And now let us consider the most common judgment trap in which all of us have participated—judging other people.

The Fallacy of Judging Another Person

Folk wisdom tells us:

Before you judge me, walk in my moccasins for thirty days.

Since you cannot walk in my moccasins for even five minutes, the admonition is that you cannot judge me. It would not even help if you could walk in my boots for sixty years!

For us to attempt to judge whether a person is right or wrong, good or bad, better or worse, is to assume an ability we do not have. If for no other reason, we cannot know what happens next. **Additionally, we cannot know the impact of our judgment on everyone and everything involved in any way, now and for all time to come.**

A Case in Point

By all of the accepted standards and required credits, I should never have been graduated from high school. However, I was graduated in 1950. Anyone who knew of my lack of academic achievement (at or near the bottom of the class with several incomplete subjects) might well have said, "The boy can be a cowboy or handle some other blue collar job, but he won't succeed in any job requiring basic academic skills."

If a person had made such a judgment, they would have been incorrect. They could not know of an event that would happen in 1957 that would create a desire for learning in me and forever change my life. By my definition I became a continuous student.

At the time I was employed as a blue collar telephone company employee in the mountain town of Salida, Colorado. One afternoon my manager said, "Bud, there is an adult education course coming to town, and this evening there is a demonstration meeting. Why don't you come with me?"

I did, and the next day I went to the bank and borrowed $160.00 for the tuition to participate in a Dale Carnegie Human Relations Course. Without being aware of it, I was ready to learn, and the things I learned in that course changed my life.

Let me reinforce the idea of the fallacy of judging people with the following scenario. My son, Michael, had always been a good student until he entered middle school. Then he fell off the academic wagon. His mother and I attended several meetings with concerned teachers, counselors, and the school principal. I was strongly encouraged to bring pressure on Michael to improve his academic standing. I am capable of doing that. I have proven it to myself on numerous occasions. But subsequent learning has taught me that leaning on someone to force compliance is not a good course of action. Almost always it is counterproductive. Even if I could force academic achievement, what would be the cost in terms of side effects?

My strongly held objective was to make a good decision for Michael. Being well aware that I do not have all the answers and I could so very easily make a decision I would later regret, I turned to my spiritual Teacher and sought guidance. I prayed and meditated on the subject for the next several mornings. (At that time, with a busy professional and family schedule, I carved out my alone time by arising an hour before anyone else in the house and going to my quiet place.)

Considering my limited knowledge and ability regarding such things, meditation to me is just being as mentally and physically quiet as I can for some minutes after prayer. (I have read that I should continue to sit as quietly as possible for at least two or three minutes after I first think it's time to stop.)

After meditating there are times I sense an impulse to write. After several meditations, wherein part of the focus was my son's situation, I had such an inclination. I wrote as follows:

> *Do not risk your relationship with Michael in order to force academic achievement. You are not capable of judging the impact of academic achievement or lack thereof on his life.*

Where did the message come from? Certainly an argument could be made that it came from my conscious or subconscious mind. But does it really matter? The doubts, which were fears, had disappeared. It was then I had the electrifying experience of knowing a deep truth. I remembered my own lack of academic achievement and knew I could not know what would happen next to Michael. I realized I was incapable of judging Michael's situaion.

(*NOTE:* Five years later, as this is being written, Michael is a freshmen attending a Colorado state college, with a grade point average of 3.4.)

One of the activities I maintained during those years was seeking guidance on how to help my son and other members of my family. I was often guided to encourage them, **never to criticize them.** Because of my fallibility and very imperfect ways, I need all the help I can get. I so wish in my life I had never criticized any member of my family or any other person. I shudder to think how I would have handled Michael's situation without guidance.

I profoundly believe I was guided to remove him from the public school system. I am very grateful I could offer him the opportunity to attend a private high school, which had rigid academic requirements, and that he accepted the offer. Through meditation and prayer, I was assured that the significant expense of the private school was the best investment my wife and I could make in our son's future.

One of the major reasons we cannot judge situations accurately is because we cannot know what happens next.

Releasing Judgment of People

If one chooses to be God's teacher and advance in terms of effectiveness, one must strive to stop judging people. Perhaps a starting place is to begin with the very simple statement, "He or she is different from me." The indisputable reality is that in the history of the world there has never been another human being just like you. However, no matter whom we compare ourselves with, if we focus on our similarities rather than our differences, we will find that we are much more similar than different. If we understand our differences and celebrate them, rather than fear them, we can learn from each other and become friends rather than adversaries.

If we choose to strive to give up judgment of others, we can start very close to home. It is common for Roman Catholics to believe Baptists are wrong and vice versa. The same can be said for Christians and Jews, or Buddhists and Muslims, or believers and nonbelievers, or Democrats and Republicans. It goes far beyond charity to adopt the mental position that while people may be different from us that doesn't make them wrong. **Without judgment, prejudice disappears.**

It is important to keep in mind we are not talking about decision making here. We are talking about judging people. We may make a decision to avoid associating with someone because of perceived differences that make us uncomfortable. This decision can be made with no judgment whatsoever regarding who is right and who is wrong or who is good and who is bad. Where values are concerned the simple law is:

Like attracts like and opposites repel.

My value system leads me away from associating with people who do drugs. However, I am no more capable of judging the rightness or wrongness of their behavior than are those who may judge me for enjoying Scotch Whiskey or Cabernet Sauvignon wine (room temperature, of course) with my dinner.

Life is a school, and I cannot know what lessons another may need to learn for him or her to proceed upward on the path toward oneness with God. I don't even know the lessons I need to learn! It is also comforting to believe that the door that leads to rejoining our Creator is never closed to any human soul. In this belief it is not a matter of whether any soul will rejoin God, it is just a matter of when. *A Course in Miracles* tells us that judgment and love are opposites. From judgments come all of the sorrows of the world. But from love comes the peace of God.

A Most Difficult Decision

The awareness that I wanted to become one of God's teachers and that to do so I must work at giving up judgment came at an opportune time in my life. For several years I had been a member of a personal growth group consisting of six men. We met monthly for four or five hours, and at least two or three times a year we had a weekend retreat. The group existed for eight years. The love relationships it cemented will last throughout my life.

One of the commitments each of us agreed to was to serve as a personal growth consultant to the other members. We called ourselves the PGA—Personal Growth Associates.

During one especially powerful retreat weekend I received, understood, and accepted the feedback that during the retreat I had been very judgmental. This, of course, was not the first time I had received such feedback, but it was the first time I was clear on the pain I had caused. I clearly saw the destructiveness of my judgmental statements. It was then I decided I wanted to change and become more accepting of others and learn to avoid judging them.

I was earnestly searching for means to become less judgmental when I started studying *A Course in Miracles*. It contains priceless information regarding judgment. This timely discovery lead me to become a serious student of the *Course*.

Shortly after becoming excited about the newly found source of wonderfully practical information, I came face to face with a shockingly difficult requirement I had to deal with if I wanted to become one of God's teachers. **The *Course* was very clear, not only must I strive to be nonjudgmental, I must also strive to turn over decision making to my Higher Power!**

This was very upsetting to me. As explained in the *Course*, it is a slow process, not because it is particularly difficult, but because it is apt to be personally insulting. A primary objective of our educational system is to prepare us to use logic and factual information to make decisions. This requirement was a direct reversal of all of the education and training I had had in my life! For some time I was not sure I was willing to try to make that adjustment in my behavior.

Decision-Making Reality

I now understand that no human being makes a decision by himself or herself anyway. We always collaborate with our **love side or our fear side.** This information was very comforting to me, especially when I understood it more fully and had tested it to my satisfaction. It is perhaps easier for us to accept, if we can visualize the cartoon in which the protagonist, who must make a decision, has an angel on one shoulder and a devil on the other.

The angel of course, is inputting love-based messages, such as: "Be kind. Be generous. Be forgiving. Be patient. Be trusting." While in the other ear the fear-based messages are: "Get even. Take all you can get. Now is your chance. Don't give in. Don't trust them."

The real question is, will you collaborate with your love side and the Holy Spirit, or will you collaborate with your fear side, your ego? It is one or the other. There is no middle ground and, it is a matter of personal choice!

Again, let me encourage you to consider that **love** and **fear** are opposites and co-variables. If one increases, the other automatically decreases. We know we cannot be afraid and loving at the same time. Likewise, we cannot be fearful and trusting at the same time. It is also true we cannot be happy while we are afraid, just as we cannot be loving and jealous, or loving and suspicious, at the same time. And the comparisons can go on and on, *ad infinitum.*

All of us want to be happy in our lives. Happiness is a love-based condition; therefore, if we want to be happier we must learn to live with less fear.

✧ **If we live with more love, we live with less fear.**

✧ **If we make more love-based decisions, we live with less fear.**

✧ **If we live with less fear, we are happier.**

There are wealthy people in our society who by their own public admission are greedy. This teaching tells us they can never be truly happy and have peace in their lives until and unless they overcome this fear-based condition.

It has long been known that our ability to love others is dependent upon our ability to love ourselves. In truth you cannot even love your mate or your children if you don't love yourself. Oh, yes, you may be very accommodating to them and fulfill their every physical and psychological need because of your responsibility. But to love them is to fulfill a spiritual need! It emanates from the love of God who admonishes us to love our neighbor and ourself!

What kinds of things must we do to learn to love ourselves? The following question may provide a starting point:

When do you love yourself the most, just after having been greedy; or just after having been generous?

The Giver

Some psychologists have strange and perhaps uncomplimentary things to say about people who collect things. In spite of those so-called learned opinions most of us are, or have been, collectors of something.

In my youth I had a collection of rifle ammunition and another of mineral samples. Later I collected antique bottles that I dug from the refuse dumps of Colorado ghost towns. Perhaps my most interesting collection (and the only one of which I have some remnants) was of Native American artifacts. I have not added to this collection for many years. However, I frequently think of one major lesson this hobby brought to me.

I was conducting management training classes in El Paso, Texas, on a regular basis. Each trip was two weeks long. I usually spent the interim weekend pursuing my hobby of collecting artifacts.

After I became friends with some of the locals who participated in the training classes, they invited me to go with them on a weekend expedition into Mexico. The organizers of the outing were after some good old R and R—in this case raucous rowdyism. But for me it was an opportunity to hunt artifacts in an area rich in Indian history.

I found and was able to bring home several beautiful pieces—stone ax heads and matate and mono stones (used to grind grain). But I failed to find a prized *olla* (pronounced oh-ya), or bowl, for which these Indians were noted.

When we returned to El Paso one Sunday evening, one of my hosts invited me to view his collection of *ollas* and other artifacts. He escorted me to the game room

WHO IS THE GIVER?

I won't complain about the past;
the future I don't know.
But just today I think I see
forever in the glow.

The chance for us to learn and grow
is always opportune.
Tomorrow is just a breath away
and is yesterday so soon.

But time we have in like amount
each one the stated moment,
for each of us a separate route
along life's path intent.

We stress ourselves and waste and fret
and miss the beauty known,
and rush right past the quiet part
and wonder what went wrong.

But time there is to do our task
and love the life we're living.
We have enough and will complete
if we can learn of giving.

Who is the giver,
he who could divest?
Or he who is receiving
with thanks he can express?

in his basement. There before me on two shelves were several of the most magnificent *ollas* I had ever seen, along with some very plain and drab ones. I picked up and admired a fine dark one that had a beautiful patina and was intricately carved. After I placed it back on the shelf and examined the others, including the drab ones, my friend said, "Bud, I'd like you to pick one you would really like to have."

He knew as well as I which one I liked. His smiling face, eyes atwinkle with expected pleasure, fell when I selected one of the colorless, drab bowls. I realized instantly what I had done. But it was too late. I had denied my friend the joy of giving me a cherished gift.

Sometimes psychological hang-ups we put on ourselves during our formative years change slowly. Yet there are other times when, with lightning speed, learning happens. This was one of those times.

Testing Spirituality
Option I

It is my contention that spirituality is practical, not a pie in the sky myth. If that is true and if it is indeed practical, it is appropriate to test it—to see if, in fact, it will be useful to me. Yet, just as with testing anything one must give it a fair trial.

The following process will enable you to evaluate the usefulness of striving to make all of your decisions from a love base rather than a fear base. (It was fear that caused me to select the drab *olla*.)

It is a given that all of us would like to have more ideal days. An ideal day is one in which we are able to accomplish our tasks and experience some of our desires. The process for experimenting with this concept is as follows:

*At the beginning of your day make a list of
the things you want to happen that day under
the heading of my ideal day. Be as specific as
you can.* Then make the commitment to consciously strive to make love-based decisions,
**every time you must make a decision
that day—from the most mundane to the
most impactful. There are times you
have more than one alternative and it is
not always obvious what the love-based
or right decision is. It is at these times it
is imperative to use your resources—Ask
your spiritual resource for guidance!**

This process, which is taken from *A Course in
Miracles*, tells us the spiritual promise is that if we
strive to make decisions in this manner, we are
assured of more ideal days.

I am sure many of my friends think I am a bit
wacko when I tell them of my efforts to live by this
process. For example, even when I walk into my
closet at the beginning of my day, if I am not very
clear on what I should wear, I ask for guidance. I
can't explain it, but the clothes just seem to jump off
the hangers!

Does this mean that for every decision we make we
should ask for guidance? **No!** When we **know** what to
do, **just do it!** But when we don't know, **ask!**

When you have completed a reasonable test period (about three weeks), you will have proven to
yourself that striving to live by love is much more
satisfying than living and being guided by fear. If you
adopt this more effective way of making decisions,
the spiritual promise is that you will be led to a more
joyful way of living.

Option II

If you are really serious about this business of living a happier, more peaceful life by utilizing your spirituality, give the following activity a thirty-day test—a fair trial:

Instructions: Arise thirty minutes earlier than other members of your household and use your time in the following manner:

✧ Five minutes to go to a quiet place
(Use the same place every day.)

✧ Five minutes to thank God for your blessings

✧ Five minutes to ask God to help you **live, love, listen, learn, and laugh in His light this day**

✧ Five minutes to ask God five questions and make one statement:

"What do You want me to think today, God?"

"What do You want me to do today, God?"

"Where do You want me to go today?"

"What do You want me to say today?"

"To whom do you want me to say it?"

"When I don't know, please decide for me."

✧ Eight minutes to sit quietly and be receptive

✧ Two minutes to go to the kitchen and make the coffee and get ready to have a ten day

A Random Sample of Miracles

"Where do you want me to go today, God?"

I had just returned home from a lecturing and consulting trip of several days. It was early on a Friday evening. As soon as I had set my suitcase down and hugged the family members who were home, my wife, Judy, said, "We have a decision to make." I asked her what was going on. She replied she had received a call that morning from one of the organizers of a meditation breakfast for the following morning in San Francisco.

A dear friend of ours has a debilitating disease that is quite serious. A group of her friends had organized the event and initially were unaware of our relationship with the honoree. They apologized for the short notice but strongly encouraged us to participate.

I asked Judy what she wanted to do, and she said it really didn't matter to her. "What do you want to do?" she asked.

I didn't have a preference either. I'm sure almost everyone has experienced a dilemma such as this. We did have plans for the weekend, but nothing that couldn't be easily changed, and money was not a problem. We certainly did want to see our friend, but we were really struggling with the decision, and we had to decide quickly if we were to catch the last flight that evening to San Francisco.

After several minutes of no-progress, we decided to give the decision to God. Within seconds the light came on. The message was, "Call our friend and ask her!"

Judy immediately dialed her and she said, "Oh, no, don't come now. Come next weekend when it will just be the three of us!"

"What do you want me to say today, God?" "To whom do you want me to say it?"

✦ It was a normal busy day at my desk after an absence of over a week on a lecture tour. The mail included the courtesy membership roster of a dental study club to which I had lectured a year or so earlier.

As I absentmindedly thumbed through it, I came across a name I recognized, and I immediately had a very strong premonition to call the person. After I dialed the man's business number, his wife answered. When I announced who I was, she started crying and said, "Bud, how did you know we needed to talk to you?" I quickly asked her, "What's going on?" She told me that just an hour before her and her husband's worst fears were confirmed. He had inoperable brain cancer and could no longer practice dentistry. I talked to both of them for about the next hour. I know I was directed to call them, and I know that my intervention was useful.

✧ A few days before Christmas I was sitting at my desk, looking forward to a week of greatly reduced activity. Suddenly I received the internally generated motivation to call the home of a client/friend in Texas. His wife answered the phone. When she heard my voice, she was almost speechless. She said, "Not more than two minutes ago I was holding a picture of you and my son as you were teaching him to use the fishing rod you bought him. I said I so wished I could talk to you. How did you know?"

✧ I called a friend in Brattleboro, Massachusetts, because of a gentle but persistent internal urging. I caught him just as he was leaving his office to attend a meeting. He was extremely angry. After we visited for a couple of minutes, I asked him what he wanted the result of the meeting to be. After he explained the situation, I also asked him if he was willing to risk the loss of his relationship with long-term associates because of ego- and fear-based anger? He also asked how I knew he needed to talk to me.

These incidents and many more like them continue to happen. This is not to suggest they happen to me every day. However, they happened very rarely prior to the time I faithfully began asking God, every day, what He wants me to think, what He wants me to do, where He wants me to go, what He wants me to say, and to whom.

To live our lives according to this plan is very simple indeed. Proceed without question when you know the right thing to do. If there is a question regarding what is the right course of action, just ask.

VICARIOUS ENERGY

There are some places I have seen
where beauty is all sublime;
The trees and grass and water blend
into a view entwined.

With scented air and clear blue sky
and peace on every hand,
Wild flowers in profusion grow
and gaily cover the land.

A heavy heart when walking there
if only in mind's eye,
Finds faith renewed and love to share
and courage again to try.

Chapter Five

GAINING THE ENERGY TO SOLVE OUR PROBLEMS

*The only learning from successfully solving
a problem is how to solve the problem, not the
elimination of the problem. The problem is
eliminated—leaves us never to return—when we
learn the lesson behind the problem, which is the
reason we had the problem. We will then advance to
another opportunity for growth (we can cease to
refer to these incidents as "problems") and it will be
easier to solve the new one and learn from it
because of our progress.*

❖ ❖ ❖

*Growth can begin when we have awareness
of some behavior we wish to change
and own the behavior with discontent.*

❖ ❖ ❖

*The key to freeing love's power begins with
forgiveness. To forgive ourselves and all others
is congruent with God's teaching and allows
His love to work miracles in our daily lives.*

A Philosophy of Growth

Education occurs when we mentally accumulate information.

Learning occurs when we apply this information and determine its usefulness or lack thereof.

Growth occurs when we have tested the information, found it useful, altered our way of thinking about our world, and made positive changes in what we think, causing us to change what we do and what we say.

> ✧ When growth occurs, it does so according to the timetable of the learner not the teacher. Teachers can only provide the opportunity for growth.
> ✧ Growth is volitional. It occurs naturally from internal desire, not external pressure.
> ✧ Growth is greatly facilitated by faith, because growth is change and change brings risk.
> ✧ Growth is facilitated by love. Fear blocks it.

Whatever else we may say or think about education, learning, and growth, if we choose to grow we can be sure there will be an increased requirement for energy. We can build a strong case that growth is not complicated, but since it is difficult, it will indeed require energy.

The Energy Pool

It is helpful if we accept the concept that we have a finite amount of energy at any point in time, a pool of energy. We re-energize our pool (recharge our batteries) with sleep, rest, nourishment, and recreation.

On a typical day, as our day progresses, our supply of energy decreases. It will be helpful if we can agree that there are at least three different kinds of energy in our energy reserve or pool. The three types of energy we shall consider are:

✧ Physical Energy
✧ Mental Energy
✧ Love Energy

Physical Energy

It is not the purpose of this book to explore in detail the readily available information regarding exercise, diet, nutrition, rest, and recreation. But it is within the scope and purpose of this book to discuss physical energy as it relates to our ability to be a more loving, more fully functioning person.

There is a little known factor in our lives that is phenomenally influenced by our level of physical energy. That factor or element of our behavior is our tolerance for disagreement. Our ability to cope effectively with disagreement, or anything that happens outside our zone of expectation, is greatly reduced when we are physically tired.

Please attempt to recall the last time you lost emotional control. It was probably in the afternoon or evening or at some other time when you were physically tired. When we are physically tired, we are weaker and feel more vulnerable. It is important to accept that you are much more susceptible to reacting defensively to a given situation when your physical energy reserve is lower.

Now take a few minutes to review *Diagram 2*. The chart is designed to graphically portray the correlation between a high level of goal achievement,

2. THE RELATIONSHIP OF

NUTRITION • EXERCISE • PHYSICAL ENDURANCE
TOLERANCE FOR DISAGREEMENT • GOAL ACHIEVEMENT PROBABILITY

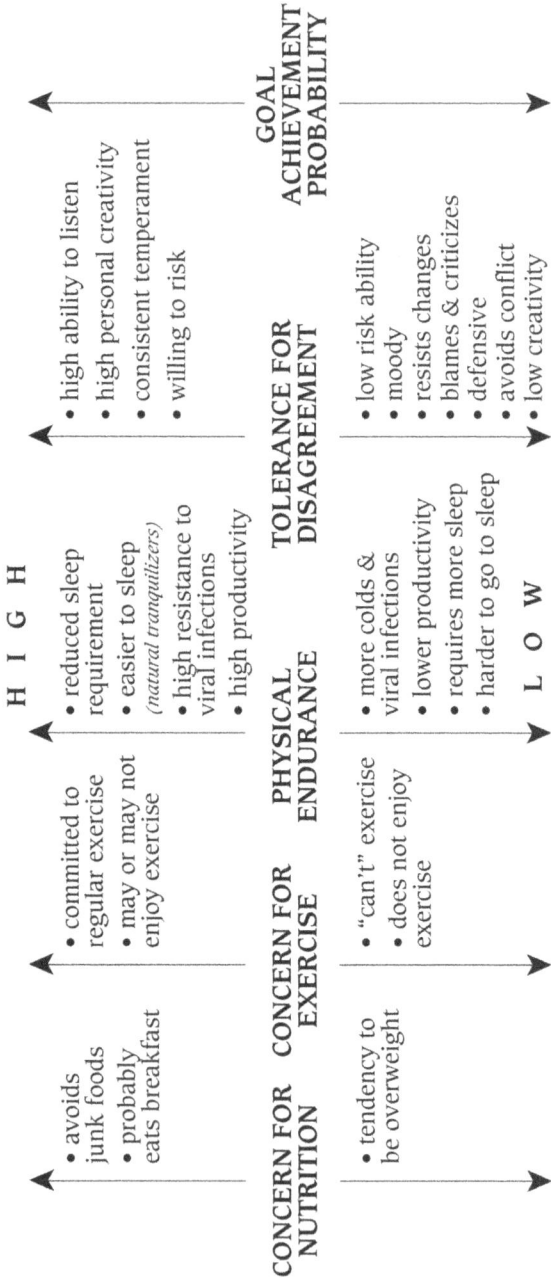

CONCERN FOR NUTRITION	CONCERN FOR EXERCISE	PHYSICAL ENDURANCE	TOLERANCE FOR DISAGREEMENT	GOAL ACHIEVEMENT PROBABILITY
HIGH				
• avoids junk foods • probably eats breakfast	• committed to regular exercise • may or may not enjoy exercise	• reduced sleep requirement • easier to sleep *(natural tranquilizers)* • high resistance to viral infections • high productivity	• high ability to listen • high personal creativity • consistent temperament • willing to risk	
LOW				
• tendency to be overweight	• "can't" exercise • does not enjoy exercise	• more colds & viral infections • lower productivity • requires more sleep • harder to go to sleep	• low risk ability • moody • resists changes • blames & criticizes • defensive • avoids conflict • low creativity	

which we all desire, and our level of physical strength. In short, when we are physically weaker, we are more vulnerable and therefore more defensive, which works against goal achievement.

Physical Energy and Goal Achievement

If our concern for nutrition is high, we probably avoid junk foods, we are temperate in what we drink, and we probably eat breakfast. If our concern for physical endurance is high, we probably exercise. If we have a regular exercise regimen and are prudent with what and how much we eat and drink, there are observable benefits. We are likely to have a reduced sleep requirement, and it is probably easier for us to go to sleep because of the natural tranquilizers exercise produces. We will also have a higher resistance to viral infections and will be more productive.

There are indeed many benefits or payoffs for high physical endurance. Perhaps the greatest of these is an increased **tolerance for disagreement.** Some of the resulting benefits are:

⋄ An increased ability to listen, especially to things we don't want to hear
⋄ A more consistent temperament
⋄ An increased ability to confront without defensiveness
⋄ A greater willingness to risk
⋄ An increased level of personal creativity

When we are in possession of a more amiable disposition, others will be much more inclined to be cooperative and be open and honest with us. These factors, when combined with increased personal creativity, greatly enhance personal goal achievement. All considered, these are strong reasons to increase our level of physical energy. When increased **tolerance for disagreement** is added to the other reasons we have for maintaining our physical bodies, it can cause us to reevaluate our commitment to that process.

Mental Energy

We are going to explore ways of increasing PMA—Positive Mental Attitude. Quite obviously this is a necessary component to being a happy, healthy, productive person. I have many people to thank for contributing to my brand of PMA; Jesus, Norman Vincent Peale, Harold Wirth, Earl Nightingale, James Allen, Michael Vance, Norman Cousins, and my mother, to name a few.

Pessimism, which is a negative mental attitude, is a fear-based mental state and as such is a waste of time and energy. It is love-based optimism that enables mankind to progress toward the spiritual being that we truly are.

Pessimism is a choice, a fear-based choice. Pessimists tend to believe in fate, luck, and powerful others and to believe that they are relatively powerless to influence their own destiny. When coupled with cynicism, which is often the case, the pessimist/cynic not only ceases to trust others but finally ceases to trust himself or herself, a severe penalty indeed. These individuals are referred to as "externals" because they believe their lives are controlled by forces external to themselves.

For us to attain and retain an optimistic attitude, it is not necessary for us to have an unrealistic, Pollyannaish view of the world and humankind. It is helpful, however, if we believe people do have a noble, God-endowed spirit and there is a continuous, never ending scenario of man's goodness to his fellow man. We must seek out this goodness, for as we shall review later, the media does not often focus on the positive.

Being an optimist is also a choice. Optimists are internally directed (therefore referred to as "internals") and know their effort makes a difference. For this reason they tend to be much more successful in life. They are motivated to put out great effort, for they believe they will be rewarded. Among other things they are happier, more trusting, have more friends and live longer. This style of thinking contributes to their feelings of self-worth. It is much easier for them to believe they will be rewarded in life according to what they think they are worth and that their feelings of self-worth will greatly influence what the world thinks they are worth.

Negative Bombardment

Several years ago my wife and I were returning to Denver from a business trip to the Northeast. There was about a two-hour delay during a plane change in Chicago. We entered the United Airlines club room, and as my wife went to the telephone to check in with our children, I sat down and began watching a television program. At the beginning of the program I was calm, quiet, and at peace with the world. In a matter of seconds I was in a rage. I wanted to attack!

The opening scene in this "entertainment" was a woman in her night clothes, lying asleep on her bed. The moonlight was streaming into the room and the wind was gently blowing the lace curtains. In the next scene a man climbed through the open window, held a knife to her throat, and raped her!

My feeling of equanimity and sense of being at peace with the world was shattered. Is that entertainment? Is that good for me?

In our modern society with all of the communications advancements, we are bombarded continuously with violence and negativism in the media of radio, television, and the press. If we do not diligently and deliberately reduce or dilute that flood of negativity, our minds and thinking will become polluted and unbalanced by the tragic, the sad, and the fearful events in the world. When this happens, pessimism, with all of its penalties, becomes the most likely mind-set.

It is quite well established that we do have a subconscious mind. The function of the subconscious mind is to record and file away everything we experience, including our thinking. A useful analogy is for us to think of our subconscious as a pool that does not have a drain. We can only put information into it. We can remove nothing.

In our negative, fear-based society the daily input into our pool, from which we can remove nothing, is heavily overbalanced with ugly, sad, violent, negative, punitive, and tragic information. Unless we make a determined effort, the pH of our subconscious pool will inevitably become unbalanced toward the negative.

About thirty years ago Maxwell Maltz's very useful book *Psycho-Cybernetics* was published. His research and experience clearly made the case that our subconscious mind functions much like a computer. We program our computer with our thinking, which is most greatly influenced by what we experience. According to Maltz, we are programming our mental computers to create unhappy futures for ourselves if we spend much of our time experiencing violence, tragedy, sadness, man's inhumanity to man, and other forms of ugliness. Our primary exposure to such negativity is through movies, television, and newspapers.

There is growing awareness that violence in the world is significantly fueled by violence in what is labeled as entertainment. One study indicated the average twenty-year-old American has seen 19,000 murders in his or her lifetime. To the subconscious mind, a murder is a murder. It does not differentiate between a staged murder and an actual one. Clearly the media is negatively influencing the pH of our subconscious pools.

Citizenship and Responsibility

We seem to have a dilemma here. On the one hand, if we want to be informed, responsible, actively participating citizens, we must rely on the media. On the other hand, if we wish to be joyful, positive, and optimistic, the media works against us. What are we to do when we must rely on the negatively biased media for necessary information?

Please consider the key word in the last sentence as "necessary." To reverse the negative pH in our subconscious pool and still be informed, **we must decide what we put into our pool by not only avoiding entertainment depicting violence, but we must also edit the news!** But how, you may ask, can we edit television and radio news? You can't, but you can edit your newspaper!

Give yourself a break. Test the theory! For a thirty-day period strive to totally avoid the broadcast media news programs! This would also be an ideal time to begin keeping a daily feelings journal. If you decide you **want** to be a more optimistic person, this simple, though not easy, change in your daily regimen can indeed make a positive difference.

By reading the headlines of articles in the newspaper you can edit out and refuse to read those articles you do not need to know about or don't want to know about. Can you, or the world, possibly benefit from you reading the gory details about a deranged father who knifed his four children to death and then took his own life? Stories such as this are commonplace and you can choose not to read them and thus avoid adding that bit of tragic, negative information to your subconscious pool.

I suggest you read the newspaper articles you want to know about, or think you need to know about in the early evening, never in the morning. If you must read something in the morning, read something uplifting and positive. If you must listen to something in the morning, listen to your favorite music or a tape with a positive message. Don't start your day off with a downer dose of negativity! And don't close your day that way either. Isn't that precisely what we do when we watch the late evening news? Is it any wonder we do not sleep well?

If we want to be happier, more positive people we will further our own interests if we cease to watch television programs and movies depicting violence, tragedy, mayhem, and genocide. We can seek instead the entertainment that uplifts us and has redeeming value. Our choices today, regarding home entertainment, are infinitely greater than they were just a few years ago. With the advent of VCRs and videocassettes we can exercise significant control over what we experience on the television set. Carefully selected videos can be a tremendous source of positive reinforcement.

With these simple choices we can begin to change the pH in our subconscious pools from negative to positive. With a more positive outlook on life we can awake every morning and thank God for another day and really mean it.

In the novel *The Milagro Beanfield War*, about life in a small town in southern Colorado my favorite character is Amarante. He is a very old, very fat, silver haired, nearly blind man of Mexican ancestry. All of the townspeople think he is crazy because of his conversations with Garcia, who has been dead for some time. But the reader knows Garcia's spirit is just waiting for his old friend to die so they can go off to their next lives together.

Every morning when Amarante awakes, before he opens his eyes, he carefully moves his arms at right angles to his body until they are fully extended. Then he exclaims with gusto, "Ahhh, no box! Thanks be to God for one more day!"

To help us come to the reality that each day is a gift it may be helpful to read one more page of the newspaper—the obituary page. Almost every day there will be an obituary for someone who died who was younger than you! Each day is a gift!

Love Energy

Lost Years

After an estrangement of over twenty years I realized I had important unfinished business with my father. I had just recently begun working in the human potential movement and had been appointed management communications consultant in the Mountain Bell Telephone Company. In that capacity I had become a serious student of human nature. I was further motivated to complete this unfinished businesses by the realization that my father's chronic emphysema had become acute and would claim his life.

When I was in my early teen years, my father had an affair with another woman for about a year. He would return home at two or three o'clock in the morning. I never went to sleep until his car lights shined on my bedroom window as he turned into our driveway. Many nights I heard my mother crying herself to sleep. Sometimes I heard the terrible arguments.

Until that happened, I had my father on a pedestal. I know now he could not possibly have lived up to the image I had of him. As a consequence of the lofty position he held in my mind, when he fell, he fell extremely hard. For the next twenty-two years we were not friends. But as my father's death appeared imminent, I wanted to make peace with him.

My mother was fortuitously absent the evening I selected for the visit. I prepared our dinner, and the conversation about mundane things was comfortable. After dinner I disclosed my hidden agenda. I told him my purpose in coming was to forgive him for the affair of years ago. I told him as a grown man I could understand how such a thing could happen and that I no longer had any anger and held no grudge. We both cried.

From then until his death we were friends again, and I visited him frequently. We went fishing one last time. Years earlier, before the estrangement, we had enjoyed many happy hours of fishing and hunting together.

Only recently have I come to the full realization that he made many attempts toward reconciliation during those years of estrangement. I rejected them. During that period of my father's life his passion was prospecting in the Colorado mountains for gold, silver, and rare earths, such as uranium. As each claim failed to produce a profit, he became more convinced the next one would be a bonanza. As each claim was filed with the county clerk and recorder it was given a name. Many of the claims were named after me; the "Buddy #1", #2, #3, and so on. He often asked me to visit the claims with him and his partner, a retired miner. Yes, I would do it differently if I had another chance!

When the reconciliation finally happened, I know it was important to him, but I cannot know what it meant to him in total. I do know, however, what it meant to me. It was a life-altering event. It was as if a huge, insurmountable barrier had been removed from my growth path. Only after I had forgiven him was I capable of thinking through the events of the affair and able to recognize the learning from the experience.

As I look back on my father's infidelity, an extremely painful event in my life, I know I was in the right place. I also entertain the thought that this very long and painful episode has provided me with a powerful teaching scenario that can help others. There is no question in my mind that this event greatly influenced my sexual mores. I would never suggest that premarital sex is wrong for other people, but it was for me. I assure you I have no regrets.

Generating Love Energy

Several years ago I was invited to address a faculty meeting of a university dental school. They asked me to talk to them about humanizing dental education. Dental education has a reputation of being very demeaning to students in many, perhaps most, dental schools.

I began the talk by suggesting I could tell them in a very few words—one sentence—how to greatly improve dental education. I told them this modified faculty behavior I was about to suggest would virtually eliminate the demeaning episodes that cause many students, not just dental students, to find their educational experiences disturbingly negative.

I had their rapt attention until I made the following statement, **"Never, *never, NEVER,* criticize a student again!"** Their interest in my presentation was immediately different, and some of the educators continued to pay close attention. Others wished they, or I, were somewhere else!

Criticism, no matter what words we may use to soften it or couch it, is attack. Preceding the word criticism, with the word "constructive," does not change it one iota! The words "constructive" and "criticism" are incompatible terms. Not one person you know has escaped the pain of criticism **and the subsequent reaction.**

The initial response to an attack by criticism is usually guilt, quickly followed by another response of either anger or shame. Either of these fear-based emotions demands attack. When we are angry we are inclined to attack someone else; when shamed we attack ourselves. An attack on ourselves, or someone else, is followed by guilt, which demands attack, which causes more guilt—thus begins an almost endless destructive cycle.

Attack is worthy of review. If a student becomes angry after criticism, in school whom does she attack? The perceived source of the pain, the teacher? Not likely—the other penalties are too great. Does she attack another student? That is quite possible. Perhaps she attacks someone outside the classroom. This too, is certainly a possibility. **But it is much more likely that she will attack herself!** *And that attack causes guilt, which demands more attack!*

None of us has escaped these devastating episodes in our lives. Let us first explore a cure. Later we shall address prevention and how to break this destructive cycle. We shall first seek to understand the pain more completely.

We know what the pain feels like and where we feel it—we call it hurt feelings. Please let me introduce you to another way of thinking about this pain.

Eastern religions teach of *chakras* in the body. There are seven of these, and they are identified as centers for concentration of various types of energy. The solar plexus chakra, located behind the navel, commonly referred to as the pit of the stomach is, in this teaching, where the soul resides.

Imagine how different it might be, if instead of thinking of such pain as **hurt feelings** we started thinking about it as a **wounded spirit!** Few of us would ever intentionally wound another person's spirit! When we think of such events in this new light, it is much easier for us to remember that for a wound to the spirit to heal takes much more than a good night's sleep and a tranquilizer. Sometimes the wound lasts a lifetime. One psychologist has written that the half-life of a criticism is fifty years.

John Bradshaw, one of the standouts on Educational Television's behavior programs, gives us a clear analogy. He says, "When there is a wound to the spirit that has not been healed by love and forgiveness, there is a hole in the soul allowing love energy to leak out."

Rachel Remen, a San Francisco Bay Area physician, gives us a different analogy. She says, "For every wound to our spirits, unless it is healed, there is a spot of negative energy on our hearts. This negative energy cancels out a like amount of positive energy."

Healing occurs when we rid ourselves of the spots of negative energy and the holes in our soul by forgiving the people we believe have hurt us.

Every unhealed wound to the spirit has attached to it a measure of negative energy. On numerous occasions every human being has suffered the pain of a wounded spirit. It is appalling to think of the amount of negative energy most of us carry with us wherever we go. Negative energy cancels out or neutralizes a like amount of positive energy. Now we have at least a partial answer to explain why at times we are so short of love's positive energy.

Following my presentation to the audience of dental educators, an assistant dean came up to me and said, "I can really relate to the 'negative spot on your heart theory.' Fifteen years ago a dental school educator wounded me deeply. Every time I think of the incident I become angry all over again! But what can I do about it now. He has been dead for five years."

I responded, "If you are ready, it will be a simple matter to remove the spot of negative energy by writing a letter to the deceased person. In that letter tell him everything you ever wanted to say to him, but write it in a loving way with an objective of forgiveness, not in a criticizing or attacking way. Seal the letter in an envelope with his name on it and put it in the back of one of your desk drawers. Some people believe he will receive the message, but whether he does or not isn't our concern. Our concern is to restore your love energy."

Loving Guidance: An Alternative to Criticism

After eight successful years in the Bell System on various blue collar and technical assignments, I was promoted to salesman in the marketing department. Success as a salesman required very different skills from my previous assignments.

After six months on my new job my first performance review was scheduled with my sales manager. My performance, which was measured in the dollar value of the revenue my sales generated, was mediocre. I had considerable apprehension as I entered my manager's office for the review.

The manager rose to greet me with a handshake, and after pleasantries he eliminated my anxiety by saying, "Bud, I believe you have a brilliant future with the Bell System, and I want to do all I can to help that happen sooner rather than later."

For about an hour and one half I sat by his desk as we discussed my performance. His choice of words, tone of voice, and body language convinced me I had nothing to fear. During that time he gave me five specific recommendations, which he convinced me would greatly improve my performance. More traditional managers would likely have communicated the five suggestions as five criticisms!

What I now understand, but was incapable of understanding at that time, is that my manager loved

me and wanted me to succeed. I implemented his five suggestions and my results improved dramatically. I have now labeled this method of communicating desired change as *"loving guidance."*
(Please refer to Diagram 3)

The Healing Process

It is impossible that anyone in the history of mankind has ever received too much love. The fear-based orientation of the great majority of the people in the world today blocks available supplies of love. *A Course in Miracles* teaches that every attack is, at a deeper level, a plea for love. If we can accept this, it is obvious that every newspaper is full of pleas for love every day.

Just how does one go about receiving more love? Jesus answered this most eloquently and completely in the sermon on the mount when He said, "Cast your bread upon the waters, and it will be returned to you multiplied." Most of us have difficulty with this when it comes to material things, especially money. But when it comes to love, it is easy for us to agree the way to receive more love is to give it away. For some people, however, this is the glitch.

There are times in the lives of all of us when love energy is low. There doesn't seem to be any love left to give away. We may be able to argue that this is never the case, because if there is life there is love. However, when one is burdened with an unusually difficult period in his or her life, one is so in need of love it may be the last thing he or she thinks of giving away.

I presented this concept during the first day of a two-day team building workshop. On the second day one of the participants gave me the following letter:

3. THE EMOTIONAL SCREEN

A DEFENSE MECHANISM

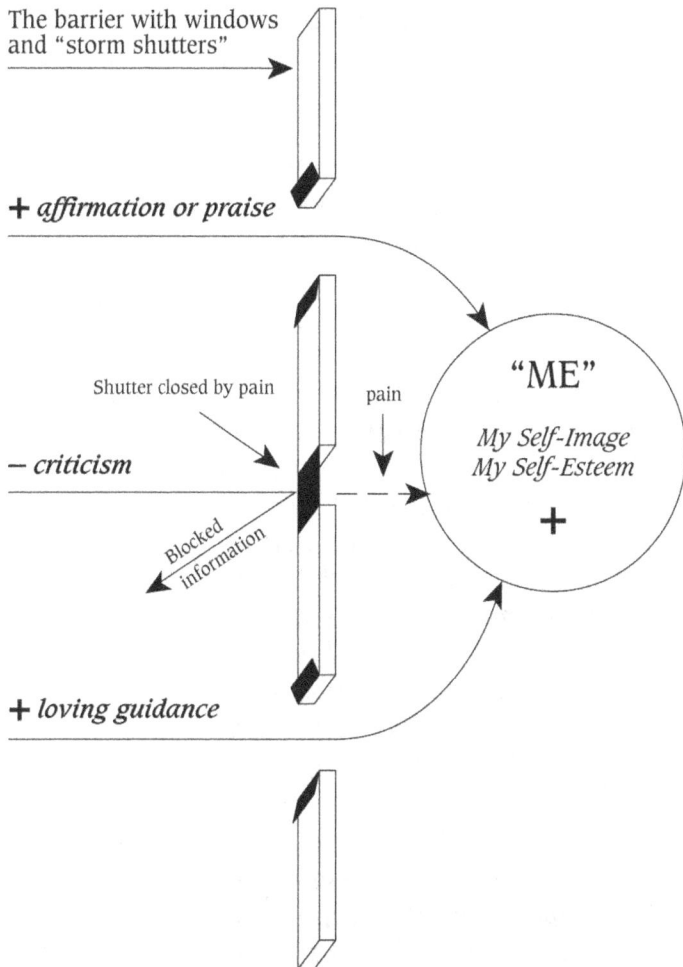

The barrier with windows
and "storm shutters"

+ *affirmation or praise*

Shutter closed by pain

pain

"ME"

My Self-Image
My Self-Esteem

+

− *criticism*

Blocked
information

+ *loving guidance*

The information content in *loving guidance* might be the same
as in *criticism*. Criticism comes from a base emotion of fear and
its derivative emotions of anger, revenge, jealousy, etc. These
negative emotions manifest as *attack*, and the probable result is
a "wounded spirit." The base emotion of *love* does not wound.

Dear Bud,

Something happened to me yesterday while sitting in your seminar, and I absolutely must share it with you.

"When the student is ready, the teacher appears." Well, there you were, telling me to make a list of all the people who've hurt me, and to write to them letters of forgiveness. Now, understand, you're not the first person who has told me of the importance of forgiving these people. Nor are you the first person who has talked about the concept of writing a letter to a deceased person. But something about the way you explained love energy, and how this hatred that I've been carrying around is robbing me of love energy touched my heart—full of black holes as it was. Well, this morning, I am pleased to report to you those black holes are all gone. The letters—all nine of them—are in envelopes in the back of my desk drawer. And I am literally blown away by this liberated feeling.

Thank you. God bless you for delivering His message of love and forgiveness. I have truly been touched by the hand of God, and I appreciate you orchestrating that event. How happy you must be in His will.

Sincerely,

Forgiveness and Health

A few years ago my wife's friend Gloria (not her real name) was preparing to leave for Montana to be near her daughter. She purchased a nearly finished home in Helena and put her home in Denver up for sale. It sold almost immediately, and she needed a place to live for a few weeks. Our home has always been an open house, and at the time we happened to have a spare bedroom, so Gloria came to live with us.

One evening after dinner, Gloria and I were enjoying a glass of wine, and she told me a very painful and personal story. Seven years earlier her husband left home one night to go to the supermarket and never returned. She went through all the agony of checking emergency rooms at hospitals, filling out missing persons reports, and visiting with police and sheriff's deputies.

Two weeks later she received a letter. He wrote that he had been having an affair with another woman and he wanted a divorce. She said she had no idea there was any problem in their marriage. For some time we talked about how devastating and painful such an event would be for anyone. Then I asked her, "Gloria, have you forgiven him?"

Her face contorted with rage, and she vehemently said, "I will never forgive him!"

I spent the next hour trying to help Gloria understand that not forgiving her ex-husband was not hurting him; but it might very well be killing her. I talked to her about the Harvard Medical School studies of several years ago that accurately predicted, to the eightieth percentile, which women would suffer cancer of the female organs within five years. They accomplished this without a physical examination or interview—just a paper and pencil questionnaire. **The prime candidate was a divorced woman who**

was bitter about life and who had few friends.

I am sure Gloria felt she had little love to give away, therefore she was getting little in return. She was a pretty woman, and she also wanted a loving man in her life. I hope I helped her see the rage she entertained and nurtured greatly reduced the possibility of that ever happening.

To Increase Love Energy (and Perhaps Prevent Cancer)

As previously stated, for spiritual people applied spirituality is practical. If this is indeed true, it is appropriate for us to test it and assess its benefits to us personally. The following process provides another means to do so.

Make a list of the names of all the people who have ever hurt you—wounded your spirit. Begin with your earliest painful memories. The list will probably be quite long. It is almost sure to contain the names of loved ones, quite likely your parents. If you do have old wounds from your parents, it is very important to place their names on the list. It is also important for you to begin to realize your parents did the best they could in their treatment of you, with their strengths and weaknesses and the events that helped shape their lives.

Step two in the process is to review the list and cross off the names of those people whom you are absolutely sure you have forgiven. Your list will probably still be quite long.

The next part of the process is to employ whatever means is acceptable to you to forgive each of the people remaining on the list. The most common way is in the quiet of your own prayer and meditation. No matter what method you choose, face-to-face, telephone call, letter, or in your own quietness, if you forgive the person genuinely with concentration and with love, once is enough. You will know forgiveness is progressing when, if you think of the incident, the memory no longer brings you pain. When forgiveness is complete, even though it is filed away in your memory bank and at times some event will bring it to your consciousness, it will be almost as if the incident never happened.

However, forgiving others, my friend, is just preliminary practice for the **main event!**

Forgiving Ourselves: The Main Event

Sin or Mistake

I was a gangly lad of fifteen years. Summer work was scarce except at home and on neighboring farms and ranches. The problem with working at home was that the pay was either very low or nonexistent. As a result I almost always had another job in addition to the daily assignments made by my father. My problem with working on farms and ranches was a severe allergic reaction to pollen and dust.

I considered it a Godsend when I was offered a job in Mrs. Jenkins' neighborhood grocery and meat market. The pay was thirty-five cents an hour, which was fifteen cents an hour less than farmers and ranchers paid. However, I was happy to accept less money and avoid hay fever.

For the first couple of months the job went smoothly. Mrs. Jenkins even talked about giving me a raise. I kept expecting to see the increase every Friday when she gave me my check. I wondered if she might raise my pay to the magnificent fifty cents an hour paid by the ranchers. I thought about it so much I convinced myself that was exactly what she had in mind. Paydays came and went, but there was no more mention of a raise even though she praised my work frequently.

I was working six hours a day, six days a week. I envisioned all the wonderful things I could do with an additional $5.40 a week. It seemed such a small sum for her I could not understand why she didn't grant the increase. Especially since I knew on a busy day we took in several hundred dollars. I was so convinced I deserved the raise I found a way to give it to myself directly from the cash register.

A few weeks later I gave up the job when school again demanded my time. I carried the guilt for nearly forty years.

Every one of us has done things we wish we hadn't—things for which we feel guilty or ashamed. It is most helpful, when seeking to forgive our own mistakes, if we have accepted the precept "Life is a school" and we realize some of our lessons are learned by making mistakes.

Let us concern ourselves briefly with semantics. For many of us who were reared in a Christian environment, the word "sin" has a powerfully negative connotation. John Wycliffe, an Englishman, translated the Latin Vulgate Bible into English in the fourteenth century. He interpreted the Latin word "peccatum" as sin. Most Latin scholars believe "mistake" is a more accurate translation.

Mistakes are learning experiences!

The following line of thinking can help you determine if it is time to forgive yourself:

While thinking about one of your mistakes for which you feel guilty, ask yourself "At this point in time do I want to do that again?" Your answer will surely be no! What we know from this simple question is that you are a more mature and wiser person now, because you made the mistake!! It is now time to complete the learning by forgiving yourself. The process is the same as for forgiving others—make a list of all the things you wish you had not done, and in your own quiet time and in your own style forgive yourself and get on with the process of becoming a whole and healed person.

It is important for you to know two things about the process of forgiving yourself:

First, you will have to battle your ego to the mat! Your ego will tell you this is a ridiculous idea, it won't work, and you don't have time for it—but if you persist, your ego will fade into the background. Secondly, you will find the list won't be nearly as long as your ego has led you to believe.

One last consideration:

*If you believe in God, you must know that He forgives you and He forgives those who you believe have hurt you. **Isn't it arrogance if you do not?***

THE ULTIMATE GIFT

Is there ought that I should do
To help another her life go through?

I'm sure there is; there has been for me
Many a person who took time to see.

The need I had, and they filled it then
With the bread of life and love again.

So thanks Great Spirit for my soul
Please use me God as Your own tool.

I thank you, God, and give me—you,
The greatest blessing I ever knew.

Chapter Six

WHERE DO I GROW FROM HERE?

Curiosity is a gift. It is always appropriate to question, sometimes silently in the quiet recesses of our mind during prayer and meditation, sometimes taking the risk of exposing our questions to the world.

✧ ✧ ✧

It is appropriate and congruent with spiritual teaching to have visions, goals, and objectives. It is inappropriate, self-defeating, and incongruent with spiritual teaching to be attached or addicted to our personally predetermined outcomes.
We are the builders, not the Architect.

✧ ✧ ✧

*Integrity is not just important, **it is everything!***

✧ ✧ ✧

To the extent we live lives of love, we live lives without fear. To be fearful of an event or a circumstance impedes love's power to heal, to correct, or to create goodness, peace, and plenty in our lives.

LIVING AND SEEKING

Overcoming Fear

One of the major missions of this book is to help as many people as possible live their lives with less fear. Man's ability to be happy has always been reduced by fear caused by superstitions, ghosts, ghouls, and goblins. Unless we have faith in a Greater Power who loves us, the most common emotional response to anything we do not understand is to fear it. A meteor shower or an eclipse of the sun or moon struck terror in the hearts of all ancient observers of these natural phenomena.

Only recently has there been information to help us understand that fear is not a necessary human emotion. This is true in spite of the fact that many people still rely on fear to guide them in difficult times and in dangerous situations. It is still very common for people to believe we can be motivated to levels of superhuman strength by fear, such as a small woman lifting a car off her husband and preventing his death. The correct analysis is that she was motivated by love. Fear immobilizes us; love enables us.

Fear of Differences

Dr. Abraham Maslow, perhaps best known for his Hierarchy of Needs concept and regarded as one of the greatest teachers of this century, also taught us the following:

> *"One of the least likely problems of a very mature, self-actualized, person is racial, religious, ethnic, or sexual prejudice."*

Many people in their adulthood entertain prejudices taught them in their youth. It is not my place to judge them as right or wrong. Yet I am quite clear that prejudice, any prejudice, is fear based and born of ignorance and reduces our peace and happiness.

If the following letter is read with an open heart and an open mind it may put love's light in the dark corners of our minds and bring us greater peace. The letter is real. Only the names have been changed. As you read the letter, it might be well to remember a spiritual law:

> ***Anything I think, or say, or do, that helps another of God's children helps me. Anything I think, or say, or do, that hurts another of God's children hurts me.***

Dear Bud,

> *Hope you are well and enjoying life. Our last personal growth meeting was really great. I feel so fortunate to be a part of it. There was so much love and learning for me, and I could see and feel it happening to everyone.*

> *Bud, you asked me a question which I did not answer, primarily because I needed some time to reflect. The question as I remember it was, "Can you help me to understand gay people?"*

> *I know two gay people very well. They are my sons, Bill and Jim. Our daughter Gloria became estranged before I learned she was gay.*

> *Both Bill and Jim tell me they knew they were gay at age six. They probably didn't know the term, but they knew their sexual orientation was different. Bill did not date girls. However,*

Jim dated several and continued dating into twenty-one or twenty-two years. He really tried to be straight, but could not find any sexual interest in women. He shared with me that his last girlfriend thought there was something wrong with her. In Bill's case he began sexual relationships with men when he started college. He also, along with Jim, used alcohol to the point I was very concerned that it was "the problem" before I learned about their sexual preference. Both boys said they never had a choice! To them it was as natural as my sexuality is for me.

Gay people are real people. They face all the same problems you and I do, plus the discrimination. Both boys have lovers, and their relationships need and get work and counseling, just like their mother's and mine.

Their life expectancy appears to be shorter, and society withholds all the support that straight couples receive. I believe they are the lepers of our society.

Although it is very different, they seem to have been made stronger in so many ways. Their work ethic standards are very high. As consumers they are very well informed. In health care, both Bill and Jim know so much more about immune system disease and drugs of choice, treatment protocol than I do.

Its in the spiritual level that I think they have reached high places. I do not see or feel any resentment for gay people, only sadness when they are the object of ridicule or discrimination.

Their caring is outstanding. As ghetto people help each other, so they support other gays. Their lives are almost completely networked within the community, but it is not exclusive. It spills over and enriches their relationships with the outside world.

Bill's former lover died of AIDS. For 1 1/2 years Bill took care of his every need. They lived together, he gave skilled nursing care, monitored his drugs, took him to the physician and hospital when needed, fed and clothed him and comforted him. David's family had disowned him. When David died, Bill was there, holding him. (After David's death we learned Bill had supported him completely, including his medical bills.) The lessons he learned and taught me are from higher places than I even knew existed.

An oppressed people will act differently. Most are doing like Bill did. A few become bizarre and dress, act, and think in very attention-getting and weird ways. These gays are unfortunately shown on TV and featured on talk shows and magazines. The public thinks it sees what gay people are like. It just isn't so.

Our family is so close, and we are blessed because it was unthinkable that we would not accept our own children and also those they love. I actually believe and feel like I have four gay sons, because Marc, Jim's lover, and Chuck, Bill's lover are as close as our own daughter in-law. In fact Ted's wife, Cheryl, is in the same place in my heart, as Marc and Chuck. We acknowledge anniversaries the same for all our couples. I can see Marc and Chuck contributing to the spiritual growth of my sons, and I'm grateful to them.

It was interesting to see how sensitive these boys were to our needs regarding any physical expression of sex. For several years they never showed any signs of affection toward their lovers. A change came last summer when we surprised Jim by going to his house on his birthday. There were about 20 gay people there, most of whom had not told their parents they were gay. As we moved about meeting and talking to Jim and Marc's friends, we were welcomed and really enjoyed meeting them. For Jim and Marc, this was real acceptance and they became gradually more open in their affection. It was a shock at first to see my son kiss another man on the lips. But the feeling in my gut was soon gone as I saw they let me in their world.

These few examples I hope can open for you, Bud, some of the windows I've seen.

The following are some truths I personally believe, and they have helped me when I get confused:

Gay people are real people, just like you and I.

Sexual choice is probably a genetic trait with many forms and then layered with environmental features.

Gays have no more choice in their sexuality than I did. I could not have restrained myself from expressing my sexual desires, i.e., being celibate. Therefore I impose no such expectation on them.

And this I feel to be true. Christ is most easily found in the poor, the outcast, and the sick. I've been privileged to see so much of Him in my sons.

Hope for the future needs to come through education, research, and the conservative church as well as the government ending their discrimination. I also know the place to start is with the individuals and the Golden Rule.

I apologize for the length and wordiness, Bud. Thanks for asking the question. As usual you helped me grow more just through this letter.

Love and Peace,

For many of us, especially heterosexual males, overcoming homophobia—the fear of our own sexuality—is indeed a very difficult task. As I was discussing this letter with a friend, he spoke of the interpretation of the Bible that tells us, "homosexuality is an abomination against God." I suggest so is adultery. Yet, if adulterers were discouraged from church membership, as gay people are in some churches, what would be the drop in membership? Perhaps the best question to ask is, "What would Jesus do?" Perhaps he would say something akin to what He said at the well, "Let him among you who is without sin cast the first stone."

A Great Fear

Perhaps one of man's greatest fears is fear of the evil one, the devil. The greatest sham in the annals of fear in mankind's history is to blame any misdirected or bad behavior on an evil influence—the devil. Yes, there is evil in the world, but it is invariably caused by man. Until man stops blaming an external entity for his misdeeds, there is a great barrier to his spiritual evolution. To fear evil is to fear ourselves. To fear the devil is to believe God is impotent. **Evil (or the devil) has no power man does not give it.**

I hope I have helped build a strong case for abandoning the fear of God. However, I do indeed believe God leaves nothing to chance. It is entirely possible Jesus' teachings would have died out in a few generations without the fear early Christians were taught to believe. It is a matter of historical fact that the vast majority of the people of that time were illiterate and very superstitious. Fear may have been absolutely necessary for His teachings to survive. That need may just as surely exist today for many of His children who persist in fearing God and believing there is an evil entity. If, in fact, fear of God is no longer necessary for the spiritual growth of others of His children, it is important they have an alternative path that just as surely leads to oneness with Him.

Brother sun, sister moon
Who are the stars, please tell.

From what I see and can perceive
I can't believe in hell—

A dreadful place of wrath and tears
where Father-Mother God

Would banish me for endless, endless,
endless years and years and years?

When we cease to fear God, there is an instantaneous and substantial reduction of all fears in our lives. If we accept the teaching of Jesus, who tells us, "All is well, have no fear, I am with you," the available further reduction of fear, which robs us of happiness, is limited only by the fears we choose to hold!

Learning and Joy from Meditation

(*NOTE:* As I mentioned earlier I am not schooled in any formal way on how to meditate. However, I am not suggesting such training would not be useful. But for me it seems quite enough, at least this point in my spiritual development, for me to be still and listen after talking to God.)

I would like to share with you another of my experiences from meditating. Several years ago I was cofacilitator at a communications and personal and spiritual growth workshop being held at an old plantation on the Mississippi River in southern Louisiana. With very little change the buildings of the plantation had been converted to a bed and breakfast and retreat center. I was housed in a former slaves' cabin for three days and two nights.

After completion of the first day's activities I was pleased to enjoy some very quiet alone time before bed. I was in the small living room reading in the comfortable, old style rocking chair. It was very peaceful, and I stopped reading for a moment to reflect on how much I had enjoyed the day and how grateful I was to be there. I also tried to think about what the walls would say if they could speak of other emotions felt in this room, one hundred and twenty-five years ago by others of God's children. Within seconds the intense emotional energy in the room caused an unanticipated flow of tears. I do not know how to describe them; they were not tears of sorrow, nor tears of joy, just tears. When the tears stopped, it was as if they caused a very comfortable and deep stillness within me. I slept very well that night.

The next night I again had time alone in the cabin. While I sat quietly, the intense but peaceful emotionality again filled the room. It was powerful and unmistakable, and I felt very safe. This time I also talked to God. I thanked Him that at least in this place slavery no longer exists. I prayed for comfort for the departed souls of my darker skinned brothers and sisters who had spent time in this same room. And then, true to my style, I became as quiet as I could. I knew I was surrounded by love energy. The following words literally flowed from my pen when I stopped meditating:

The love you teach comes not from you, but through you. It would not be right to claim or desire recognition for being a loving person because all love is God and God is all love. You are merely an instrument of God's love who has been given certain talents to teach and influence others. It is not you. Your words of peace, acceptance, compassion, joy, giving, and receiving are not your words. By letting God take over through your Angel Guides, the students who come to you for learning will receive all they can use at that time, even though each student has different needs. It is important to put your ego self aside. When you do this people will then learn to love the Source first rather than the instrument. Later they will come to love you as God's instrument.

Eliminating the Mysteries

During my lifetime I have usually found it very stimulating to think about some of life's mysteries, such as the force of energy I felt in the slaves' cabin.

And of course, at other times it has been quite frustrating. I have come to believe mysteries aren't necessarily mysterious—just something we don't understand. Said another way, there is no magic, and there really aren't any secrets—only information we may not know, or information we have not successfully applied. As a consequence we are often looking for "the secret."

The greatest truths are also the simplest. This is usually what is clarified when we finally discover the secret. Sometimes it is this very simplicity that contributes to an assumption many of us make that a concept, being simple, will be easily understood and applied.

For example, for many years I have believed the teachings of wise men, such as James Allen, and of the teachings of the ages and spiritual leaders, including Jesus and Buddha, who have taught us, **"We become what we think."** Anyone who will carefully consider personal experience can prove this to his or her own satisfaction. For example:

> ✧ If we think fearful thoughts we become afraid.
> ✧ We can literally think ourselves sick if we think thoughts of illness—psychosomatic illness is very real.
> ✧ If we tell ourselves we can't do something, we cannot.
> ✧ If we think angry thoughts we become angry and often incur the defensiveness of others.

Positive thoughts are just as powerful:

> ✧ If we think about all of the positive things we have going for us and all of our gifts or blessings, we can even overcome depression.

✧ If we think loving thoughts we communicate love.

✧ If we think happy thoughts, we become happy, and so on, and so on.

Let me state what I believe, with rare exceptions, is a very safe assumption:

All of us want to be materially prosperous.

It is also quite safe to assume, but probably not quite so obvious to us, we also want peace in our lives. That's what we're going to focus on now: obtaining peace and prosperity. Until recently that has been one of the great spiritual mysteries to me:

*"Why is the circumstance of peace **with** prosperity is so very rare?"*

A few years ago I walked a beach with a very well-known doctor who was indeed successful professionally and materially. His wife, children, and patients love him, but somehow inner peace had eluded him—there was a missing element. I so wanted to help him. But I could not. His material prosperity thinking was very good. His spiritual prosperity thinking was nonexistent.

Wealth is a relative thing; however, many people are recognized as having succeeded in their struggle for material prosperity. Some of their names are very well known. And sadly, it is also well known that many do not lead peaceful lives. Many of the troubled lives of these wealthy people who do not have peace are favorite targets of the negative press and television media. This seems especially true for individuals who have a high profile, such as well-known politicians or entertainers.

There are other people, of course, who lead lives with a relatively high level of spirituality who would define their deficiency as an absence of prosperity. For them life seems to be one financial struggle after another. If they get a few dollars ahead, their car breaks down, and they are stressed because it also needs new tires. Yet, the spiritual promise is very clear:

We should expect peace and prosperity!

That has been for me a mystery. Why are there so few people who have both?

The Path toward Peace and Prosperity

As you know, I grew up in a poor family during the Great Depression. True to form, I developed a depression mentality. I grew up with a mind-set that we live in a world of shortages. That kind of thinking convinces us there is never enough to go around. This attitude has greatly influenced my thinking and therefore my being and doing.

The marvelous book, *As a Man Thinketh*, written by James Allen in 1906, clearly convinces us, *"We become what we think."* The first step in overcoming these self-defeating attitudes is to be aware we have them and secondly, to own them with discontent. I accomplished these first two steps many years ago. And for many years I have been a very serious student of psychology, human growth and development, and communications. I thoroughly understood the change process from a psychological perspective. But try as I might, in spite of what I thought was my clear understanding, I seemed unable to rid myself of my depression mentality.

During my search for spiritual understanding, I have seen many examples of very well-meaning people, including members of my own family, who regularly attended church services, spent countless hours studying the Bible, alone or in groups, and prayed diligently. Yet, insofar as their peace and prosperity were concerned, it was obvious to themselves, or an observer, it was not working! **If they tried so very hard, why were their lives just one painful struggle after another?** It is little wonder they thought God was a punitive, vengeful entity! No question about it, their faith was great or else they would have given up many times. Their belief in reward in the afterlife—heaven—was probably all that kept them going. **But, Jesus said in the Sermon on the Mount, "Expect abundance!" Why didn't it work?**

My awareness of this seeming discrepancy, for which I did not have an answer, was a contributing factor to my first turning away and then actively rejecting God, Jesus, and all spiritual beliefs as I described in Chapter Two.

In *Sermon on the Mount*, Emmett Fox clearly helps us understand there is a test for the usefulness of spiritual activity including study, praying, and meditating. The test is, very simply, **"Does it work?"** He then helps us accept that if it isn't working we are missing something, or we are doing something we should not do, or we are not doing something we should be doing. There is ample evidence that when we strive to fulfill the teaching of love, even though imperfectly, **it does work!**

It seems obvious to me now some of Jesus' teachings are more critically important for the process to work than others—**or maybe it is just a function of where the individual student is at.**

The following is paraphrased a bit.

"Seek first to become really, really kind and loving as evidenced by what you think, say, and do and all the rest will be given to you also (absence of fear, God's peace, and material prosperity).

Let me introduce you now to more interpretations and teachings of Emmett Fox regarding this subject. Much of the following information has been extracted from his book, *Sermon on the Mount.*

To have peace and prosperity Fox recommends that first we seek spiritual prosperity. By definition we increase our level of spiritual prosperity with each and every kind and loving thought, word, and deed. It can be readily understood this contributing activity to spiritual prosperity is not limited to believers. However all of us, believers and nonbelievers alike reduce our spiritual prosperity with every unkind and unloving (fear-based) thought, word, and deed.

Many people have achieved material prosperity without achieving spiritual prosperity. However, inner peace invariably escapes them. If wealthy people believe it is only by their own efforts they have riches, it is unlikely they will gain the spiritual prosperity necessary for peace to come to them. The flip side of this is the spiritually prosperous person who cannot find material prosperity and lives in relative poverty. Peace also escapes him or her. It is very difficult to be peaceful when we cannot pay our bills!

Now let me attempt to put these thoughts together in a useful model. Please keep in mind the time-honored truth of the ages:

"We become what we think.

Thinking thoughts of poverty is no different from thinking thoughts of sickness, fear, or anger, which attract sickness, fear, or anger. Poverty thinking attracts poverty. I believe this can explain why some poor people who win lotteries remain poor. A study of the lives of lottery winners shows us that following their perceived good fortune, many of them live lives of financial disaster. (It has been reported that 93% of the lottery winners in New Zealand are in serious financial difficulty within one year after receiving the money.) Material prosperity cannot permanently come to a poor person if the winner maintains poverty thinking. Prosperity, to remain, must be made welcome by prosperity thinking! Poverty thinkers will do something, such as spending themselves into bankruptcy to cancel the peace the financial windfall could bring. Changing their thinking would eliminate the financially destructive behavior.

Certainly the inverse is true also. Materially prosperous people who do not have peace can gain it by becoming spiritually prosperous! As previously stated, one of my personal difficulties during my adult life has been overcoming what I have often referred to as my depression mentality, which is poverty thinking. For example, poverty thinking is directing my choices when I look at a dinner menu in a nice restaurant and order pasta instead of the steak I really want because the steak costs four dollars more, or buying the cheaper brand of cereal or canned goods when the one I want costs a few pennies more, or think about the price of everything before I consider its quality and value to me.

My dilemma has been I didn't know how to stop that reductive kind of thinking. Oh, I am not feeling sorry for myself—I have done well. But long ago I learned a powerful and true adage:

You cannot give from empty pockets.

Much of the good I want to do requires more than kind thoughts and words, or even physical energy. Years ago I adopted the following as one of my personal rules for living:

Be generous if there is an option, and always expect to have the wherewithal to be generous.

I like myself better when I am generous! And that includes being generous with money—**but I can't be generous with it if I don't have it!**

For several years I have been able to tell people that I now live with greatly reduced fear in my life. I attribute fear reduction in my life to striving to make love-based, rather than fear-based decisions. I now believe I have found the secret or solved the other mystery that blocks true prosperity. Poverty thinking is definitely fear based!

Now let us explore one more facet of how poverty thinking can block not only our material prosperity but also our spiritual prosperity!

A Hypothetical but Often Repeated Scenario

Two equally competent professionals practice in the same economic/geographic marketplace. One would feel very uncomfortable charging fees in the top twenty-five percent in her area and constantly struggles economically. Her neighboring professional, who does not have the hang-up of poverty thinking, has no such economic struggle.

What do you think are the most likely thought patterns of the one who constantly struggles financially? She will almost invariably adopt the attitude that we live in a world of shortages, and it is very likely she will adopt additional fear-based thinking and therefore fear-based decision making, which blocks prosperity thinking. This also reduces her ability to serve her clientele effectively.

The one who engages in fear-based financial thinking is in a very real trap. She has identifiable, tangible shortages, all the proof needed to convince herself not to expect abundance.

We know we become what we think but changing the thinking patterns of a lifetime is difficult. Yet, I can now tell you I have broken the cycle of my poverty thinking!

I believe the way to break these destructive thought patterns is to suck up your courage, deny your fear, and commit to becoming a great giver.

For years I have had people tell me that the best possible financial investment is tithing or giving part of our material treasures, especially money, to those who need it more. Usually tithing is associated with giving money to a church. That doesn't fit for me because I am not a member of any church. But, as you well know, there is no shortage of organizations and people who need money.

I now believe this commitment to giving fosters prosperity thinking. It can also unblock the channel for God's material good to flow through to us. He wants us to have both—**peace and prosperity.** Our task is to remove the blockages!

Becoming a great giver is simple; however it does require courage. This is especially true if you have over-due bills! It becomes easy and very satisfying once you get into it and the overdue bills begin to disappear.

Friend, if you have struggled for many years and other potential solutions, such as working harder, have not resulted in the desired peace and prosperity, do something different! In any facet of your life, if what you have been doing isn't working, more of the same won't fix it.

Now the toughest question: *In order to be more prosperous are you willing to risk ten percent of your income for three months?* I know it sounds crazy, but it works.

On Being a Grasshopper

A few months ago I had the life-altering experi-ence of attending a personal and spiritual growth workshop using elements of Native American spiritu-ality. The first session, a guided meditation, was a mini-version of the Native American vision quest. During the significantly longer original version the "questor" remembers any signs or symbols experi-enced or seen during the experience, and these are drawn on his ceremonial power shield. They are thought to provide insights to the seeker of knowl-edge and become his personal logo.

During the meditation I saw several images. One of the images I just couldn't wipe from my consciousness was of a large, dark blue grasshopper. So, in keeping with the custom, even though reluctantly, I finally drew it on the cardboard representing my power shield. It

WHERE DO I GROW FROM HERE? • 173

didn't have any significance I could identify at the time. However, later during a personal and private meditation its relevance became clear to me.

One day in early summer, when I was a small boy, Grandmother Ham called me from play and handed me a book. She said, "Buddy, if you will read this book this summer and tell me what's in it, I'll give you the book."

It was a book of Aesop's fables. In late summer I gave my first book report to Grandma, and she gave me the book. It was a cherished possession, especially since there were almost no books in our home. I have long believed this event, which took place before I was eight years old, provided the initial stimulus for me to become an avid reader. Fifty-four years later the gift gave again.

I clearly remember many of the stories and several of the illustrations. One of the illustrations was associated with the fable, "The Ant and the Grasshopper." It showed the grasshopper in a very relaxed position, with a large smile on his face, playing a violin. The same illustration depicted an ant dutifully carrying a very heavy load of food to his house.

In the fable, the thrifty and industrious ant, of course, is the good guy, the model of desirable behavior. The grasshopper, naturally, is the ne'er-do-well, fiddling away his opportunity to save and prepare for the winter.

What I believe the guided meditation clarified for me is that it is OK to be an ant and it is equally OK to be a grasshopper!

In my professional career I have worked with four financial consultants at one time or another. **Without exception each of them has been much more concerned with preparation for my retirement than I am!** I know I have been a source of frustration to them. I have had a feeling of inadequacy, perhaps even guilt, when I thought of my lack of interest in my pension plan. Oh, I don't want to be a burden to anyone, my children or the state, but I'm delighted that the negative energy drain is now gone—it's no big deal, but it is a relief!

A Hidden Fear

During the second day of the same workshop that facilitated me getting in touch with my "grasshopperness," I again was led to deal with an old fear that helped me clarify another very important piece of my life's puzzle. What follows is my recollection of exactly how it happened.

The last major activity of the two-session workshop was another guided meditation, not greatly different from the vision quest meditation that enabled my earlier learning. The focus of this session, however, was for the participants to identify what they would like to release.

The fifty to sixty participants were seated in a large circle. One of the facilitators placed a six-inch square swatch of red cloth and a short piece of string in front of each person. The other facilitator placed a bit of Indian tobacco on each person's square of red cloth. We were informed of the Native American ritual of releasing a self-defeating or negative thought or habit. During the meditation when the participants had identified what each wanted to release, we were to tie the string around the red cloth containing the tobacco. Then, at a later time of our own choosing, we could release the tobacco from its pouch into a stream, a fire, or the wind. This would symbolically accomplish the release.

After each participant had tied the pouch, each had the option of disclosing to the total group what they were choosing to release. All participants did so.

During the meditation I was having difficulty identifying anything I thought I wanted to release. At first I considered forgiveness. Certainly some of the greatest releases of burdens I have ever experienced have come from that activity. But I honestly could not think of anyone whom I might need to forgive. I had been working on that for some years. Likewise, I was not dissatisfied with my progress in giving up judgment of people. And for several years I had been living with significantly less fear than I ever thought possible. But as I continued to examine my remaining fears, one I had never considered before became glaringly evident.

As a by-product of growing up during the depression of the 1930s in a family that had very little money, I developed the previously mentioned depression mentality. My shock came when I realized I had also developed, in some warped way, a fear of being prosperous!

I cannot be sure, but I think I have identified two separate bits of thinking that contributed to this fear.

During my early years I was exposed to a rather commonly held belief that suggested anyone who was rich was almost certain to be dishonest and should be avoided and viewed with suspicion. When we are taught such prejudices during our formative years, they are difficult to overcome. Additionally, in my adult life, I have worked closely with some very wealthy people who have adopted an attitude that sets them apart from their peers. These particular wealthy people seem to believe that because of the power of their money, the rules and laws that apply to the rest of society do not apply to them. I think we see this occasionally among the rich and famous.

At the conscious level I know there is no correlation between wealth and being above society's laws. And certainly there is no direct connection between wealth and dishonesty. But since I realized I had that fear—fear of prosperity—I was quite clear I wanted to eliminate it from my psyche. As I tied the small pinch of Indian tobacco into a pouch I made a commitment to release this fear.

In 1987 I bought a beautiful parcel of land. It has a very healthy growth of large Ponderosa pine trees, thickets of almost impenetrable scrub oak brush, a cliff face, a beautiful meadow, and a panoramic view of the front range of the Rocky Mountains that is almost breathtaking. My wife, Judy, and I both fell in love with the land the first time we saw it. It was on this land we planned to build our home and a learning center sometime in the future. These plans never came to fruition, and the land remained undeveloped. I received a cash offer to sell the land early in 1992. Even though the money would have been very useful at the time, after prayer and meditation I turned the offer down.

Two weeks after the workshop I decided to spend the night on a secluded knoll on the land and symbolically release my fear of prosperity. I took along the tobacco pouch, a jug of water, and a sleeping bag. I arrived in late afternoon, and as the threat of a summer thunderstorm passed I sat quietly and watched a beautiful sunset. Near the end of twilight, in the gathering darkness, I built a small fire.

Sometime before midnight, after a long and very peaceful meditation, I dropped the small, red pouch into the glowing coals and watched the flames consume it and release the tobacco, and I believe, release my fear of prosperity. There was no external evidence that anything significant was happening, but deep in my being I knew it was very important.

A bit later as I snuggled in my sleeping bag, which provided warmth against the night's chill, I enjoyed the singing of two families of coyotes. I awoke in the early dawn and until full light I watched six coyote pups play their version of the game keep-away with a rabbit skin. At times they were so close I could see their eyes, perhaps no more than thirty feet away. Their obvious enjoyment of the game was a delight to see. A couple of hours later as I walked back to my truck, I felt the lightness and the joy of freedom ushered in by being rid of yet another fear.

During an early morning meditation the following week it became clear to me it was time to sell the land. I discussed it with my wife, and she concurred. I listed the land with the same real estate broker who had handled the purchase in 1987. Within two weeks he presented me with an offer for the full price I was asking.

During the closing a few weeks later, the purchaser, a man from out of state, said to me, "Mr. Ham, I understand you have an emotional attachment to the land. Perhaps you would like to know what I have planned for it."

I agreed that I would. He said, "Nothing will be built on the land. At an appropriate time I am going to donate it to the school district with the stipulation that it remain in its natural state and be used as a place for school children to study nature." I was delighted.

The combined learnings of the past year have contributed immeasurably to my peace and prosperity and have again validated the practicality of using spiritual resources.

As James Allen's book so succinctly says, "We go where our thoughts take us." No matter how successful I was in my business, no matter how hard I worked and how much wealth I produced, my fears blocked me from the prosperity that really matters—spiritual prosperity. Deep in my being I know I shall never again be afraid I will not have all I need, when I need it. When you want or need anything, from money to a lost glove to ridding yourself of a short temper, ask for help. It works.

Your Expectations

What is reasonable to expect in lifestyle improvement, if you try to live according to the spiritual principles addressed in this book? I most sincerely wish I could tell you, but I cannot. However, I can tell about another spiritual promise you can surely depend on. It is this:

If you are on the path of spiritual growth and strive to continue growing spiritually by attempting to live the law of love, you are assured your future will be better than your past.

THE RIDE HOME

We are very tired my horse and me.
The snow is deep, up to his knees.

Which way is home? I'm glad he knows.
I lost the trail a long time ago.

My body's cold and stiff and wet.
My horse is covered with ice and sweat.

We started out early, before day's light,
worked hard all day to be home by night.

We've miles to go before we sleep,
The woods are silent, dark, and deep.

In a long ago past I read the poet's line
and in my mind go to a warmer time.

I talk to my horse without even thinking.
He answers only with his steady walking.

The muffled crunch of his steady walking
is the only noise to disturb my talking.

My mind is numb with cold and night
I must hang on though I'm weak with fright.

My horse is faithful, but he wants a warm barn.
If I fall from the saddle, I'll be here alone.

He's stumbling now, and he senses my fear.
I quiet him down and pray home is near.

He falls to his knees, and the jolt nearly breaks me.
But it jars my brain, and I'm thinking more clearly.

The fear seems so real; with increased awareness
I remember the tales that prove winter is heartless.

Of men found frozen with reins still in hand
because of poor choices to buck this raw land.

Then I remember my grandfather's teaching;
We are never alone is what he was preaching.

There is One who knows our every plight.
He is on the trail with us both day and night.

His promise to us is very clear,
"Trust Me, all is well, and have no fear."

Now my horse seems stronger, and that's a good sign.
He's walking more briskly, and it wakens my mind.

I shout, "There's a light; we're riding high."
And there's our camp; there's no dying tonight.

Now it seems it didn't happen, the fear I had before,
and my horse stops with a heavy sigh just outside the door.

SOME FACT
SOME FICTION

T HREE WEEKS HAD PASSED since he had finished reading *Joshua*. A warm spring wind and several
sunny days had unlocked his truck from the snow, and
he was no longer isolated. On this particular day, as
the flow of words slowed, he decided to exercise while
he listened to his favorite Emmy Lou Harris tape.

After a full hour on the NordicTrack he wanted a
shower. He even shaved, which was no more than an
occasional occurrence. After leisurely toweling off in
front of the fire, he put on fresh underwear, a clean
shirt, and a clean pair of jeans. He felt refreshed.

He and his dog had not left the cabin for a number
of days, and it occurred to him the twenty-mile drive to
the village would be good for both of them. He could
pick up a couple of items at the store and maybe even
buy a newspaper.

Bouncing along the five miles of rough, unimproved
road in the truck he loved put him in a delightful mood.
He felt clean and fresh and started singing after they
reached the blacktop highway that led to the village.

The village consisted of a combined store with gas
pumps, a cafe, and a saloon. The long building that
housed the businesses had obviously been built at

different times by different unskilled carpenters. Each section was separated by walls with doorways between them.

After picking up a few things in the store, he waited several minutes for a clerk to appear to take his money. There was no bell to ring for service, so he walked through the doorway into the cafe. A middle-aged woman noticed him and said, "Ain't there no one in the store?"

He said he didn't think so, and she replied, "I'll take care of you then."

The cafe area with its cast-off chrome dinette sets did not look especially appealing, but he asked if they were still serving. The woman assured him they were.

He was the only patron in the cafe. The raucous laughter and loud talk, interspersed with profanity, from the saloon came through the open doorway and a pass-through window. The pass-through window saved the waitress a few steps when a customer ordered a drink.

The greasy, oversized hamburger—the Cameron Special—with everything except mustard, was delicious. The cold can of Coors Lite, along with crisp, brown, greasy french fried potatoes with the skin still on, completed the banquet.

The noise from the saloon had died down considerably, and he could hear Garth Brooks singing "Friends in Low Places." He paid the waitress, and when she returned with his change she invited him to come into the saloon to watch a contest. She explained that two local cowboys had a one hundred dollar bet on who could drink a full glass of beer, with no hands, in the shortest amount of time. He thought that might be good for a laugh, so he followed her into the saloon.

He sat at a small table against the wall and ordered a Courvoisier. When the waitress gave his order to the bartender, there was more raucous laughter, and several faces turned in his direction. It was quite obvious the eight or ten people in the saloon were all locals and he was the only outsider.

The overweight, jovial bartender who sported a huge, black moustache and a completely bald head spoke loud enough for all to hear, "Hell, Stranger, we ain't had a bottle of French booze in here since I bought this place. It's American brandy or nothin'."

He said American would be just fine.

A table in the center of the room had been selected for the contest. As the patrons gathered around the contest table, they were quite close to the stranger. A couple of ranch hands even acknowledged his presence with, "Howdy."

The contestants were both big men. One, probably about twenty-five years old, was called "The Kid" or just "Kid." The other man was about forty-five. The Kid put a one hundred dollar bill on the table and Sam, the older man, counted out five, twenty-dollar bills.

With the exception of the waitress, who was the only woman present, the group was much more drunk than sober. The contestants were seated opposite each other with a full glass of beer in front of each of them.

Tension was high, and it became quiet. The bartender announced he would count to three, and they would both pick up their glass with their teeth, drink the contents without spilling any—not even one drop—and he would declare the winner.

Much of the tension was because of the amount of money on the table. Two hundred dollars was probably more than any of them earned in a week.

The bartender started the count. Just as he said "two," Sam leaned forward and put both of his hands on the table. The Kid jumped to his feet in protest and both glasses of beer landed in Sam's lap. Sam responded amazingly fast for his inebriated condition and had a firm grip on The Kid's shirt front and bandanna neckerchief at the throat. He was preparing to hit him with a big right fist when several of the others grabbed them both to separate them. The money fell to the floor. It seemed to take an eternity for Ted the bartender, shouting profanity, to restore some semblance of order. The stranger was forgotten as the contestants were again seated in front of two full glasses of beer, this time with their hands behind their backs.

Tension again gripped everyone in the saloon. Ted began the count. As he said "three," both men picked up the glasses of beer in their teeth and tipped their heads back to drink. In their haste they both spilled some of the beer, and it ran down the front of their shirts.

"No contest" said Ted. "You both broke the no-spill rule."

There was a murmur of disgruntled chatter, and someone said, "If both broke the same rule, it's even and it's just a matter of who finished first."

Every one knew The Kid had finished at least a full second ahead of Sam. The argument raged and threatened to become violent again. For the first time the stranger noticed another table with neatly stacked piles of bills. There were many side bets.

The stranger was becoming more and more uncomfortable as violence seemed imminent. He left a $5 bill on the table for the brandy and tip and rose from his chair to walk out. He was moving toward the door when Ted said in his booming voice, "Just a minute, stranger. What we need is an impartial judge. You heard the rules, and you saw the contest, so you settle this!"

He gently tried to dissuade Ted, but the volatile crowd would have none of his excuses. It became obvious he could become the object of their belligerence.

"All right, stranger, give us a ruling," Ted ordered.

In a clear and steady voice that belied what was going on in his gut, he said, "If you all agree that the rule stated the contestants couldn't spill any beer, then the contest is invalid and there must be another one, or each can reclaim his bet and I'll declare a draw!"

One cowboy said, "We don't want no damned draw!" The agreement seemed unanimous to hold the contest again.

It was then The Kid spoke up and addressed the crowd while looking straight in the eyes of the stranger. "We don't need no goddamn stranger to tell us what's fair in Cameron, Montana. I say we both broke the no-spill rule, so that's even and I finished first, so I get the money!" With that he lunged for the two hundred dollars, which had been returned to the table.

What followed in the next few minutes would be described differently by everyone in the saloon. It became a violent barroom brawl. Fearing for his life, the stranger headed for the door.

The Kid headed him off and shouted, "Just a minute you son-of-a-bitch, you're the one that caused all of this." With that he struck the stranger on the right side of the face with an iron fist, dropping him to the floor.

The rest of the fighting stopped, almost miraculously, as they all watched to see what the stranger would do. The Kid kept his fighting stance with arms cocked to hit the stranger again.

The stranger was on his hands and knees and slowly shook his head to help clear his brain. Then he shakily rose to his feet with his hands at his sides.

"C'mon," The Kid shouted, "You coward, won't you fight back?"

There was a hush in the room as the stranger quietly said in a gentle voice, but loud enough for all to hear, "No, that's not my way now."

He looked The Kid directly in the eyes and slowly turned his head. The Kid exploded with a crashing blow, catching the stranger just below the left ear. He crumpled to the floor.

"That's enough!" Ted shouted.

All who were there had the sickening feeling that it was already too much. Blood ran out of the stranger's ears, nose, and mouth. He didn't even quiver.

"My God," the waitress screamed, "You've killed him!"

Thirty minutes later the emergency medical technician from Ennis pronounced the stranger dead. Everyone sat in stunned silence. A few minutes later the sheriff's car with the siren screaming slid into the parking lot.

The Kid sat with his back to the bar, his chin on his chest. He was ghastly pale. The sheriff completed sizing up the situation and the medical technician confirmed that the stranger was indeed dead.

Ed was returning from Ashton, Idaho, where he had just delivered a horse. As he was passing Cameron he saw the sheriff's car with red lights still flashing. He also saw his friend's distinctive black pickup truck. He braked hard and swung into the parking lot.

As Ed quickly walked through the saloon door he asked the sheriff what had happened. The sheriff's non-answer was, "Did you know him, Ed?" He pointed to the stranger still lying on the floor.

Ed's heart skipped several beats as he recognized the ashen face of his friend. He was at his friend's side in a moment and surprised himself as he bellowed, "Bill, get up!"

Everyone was shocked at Ed's order to the dead man. They stared in disbelief as the stranger's eyelids fluttered and he drew his body into the fetal position and tried to rise. Ed, the sheriff, and the medical technician helped him to a seat.

The first to speak was the waitress. "We thought you were dead," she said in a trembling voice.

His soft voice answered, "I was."

The Kid began sobbing uncontrollably.

The stranger's commitment to attempt to live by the law of love nearly cost him his life. The group stared in greater disbelief as the stranger walked over to The Kid, extended his hand, and said "No hard feelings." The law of love was introduced to Cameron, Montana.

Journal

www.ingramcontent.com/pod-product-compliance
Lightning Source LLC
Chambersburg PA
CBHW071530040426
42452CB00008B/949